M. F S.

My golden days

M. F S.

My golden days

ISBN/EAN: 9783741193118

Manufactured in Europe, USA, Canada, Australia, Japa

Cover: Foto ©Andreas Hilbeck / pixelio.de

Manufactured and distributed by brebook publishing software (www.brebook.com)

M. F S.

My golden days

MY GOLDEN DAYS.

Yellow Holly.

THINK back!—of course I do, like every one else. Back to nursery days—some pleasant, some stormy—to lessons in the old schoolroom: to holidays in summer, or at merry Christmas; to happy mornings by the seashore, when we hunted for sea-weed and raised great sand-castles for the big waves to sweep away. These and many more such times are what I think of as I sit by a cosy fire on winter nights or wander round and round the shady garden in summer twilight, with the tall trees waving in the breeze which seems to blow back to me memories of "long ago."

Would you like me to tell them? Somebody would; a small, fair-haired Somebody who—when the dolls are safe in bed, and the toys are put away—comes and seats herself opposite to me in the firelight, or hangs on my arm as I saunter in the garden (so pleased and proud that she can reach to it), and says, "Now let us talk," which means that it is not *us* at all, but *I* who am to tell tales of what I did, and thought, and wished for, when I was no older than this "Somebody."

Perhaps the most popular subject of all is Christmas-time, for it is almost inexhaustible and makes us both forget to notice how late it is getting. There are many of these merry days to tell of, for we kept high festival in my childhood's home. Oh, what a treat it was to sit up later on Christmas Eve, listening to the carol-singers who came round in that country place, sipping just a little of the hot elder wine which cook sent up; and then at last, when it was really impossible to get sentence of bed deferred, going to sleep to dream of presents and all manner of delights, and be awakened in the dead of night by the "waits." I remember that when older people complained of this visitation as a nuisance, when they declared no Christmas-box should be given to the unwelcome musicians, I used to marvel at their bad taste, for to my little ears the scraping of the violin, the twanging of the harp, and the wild blasts upon the cornet made up the sweetest harmony—sweet, because it was a part of Christmas-time.

However, my tale now is to be about yellow holly—a fine yellow holly tree, which was admired by all the neighbourhood and the pride of my mother's heart each winter.

Perhaps it had never been so thickly berried as this year of which I am going to tell, and when great heaps of evergreens were cut down for our home decorations, in vain we pleaded for even one spray of yellow holly. "It would be a sin and a shame," so the gardener said, and our mother entirely agreed with him.

So it was Christmas Eve. Laurel, bay, and bright scarlet-berried holly wreathed the pictures on the walls; the house was full of visitors, and a merry party had gathered round a blazing fire in the dining-room, talking of the past sometimes with a touch of sadness, but more often with gay, glad memories, talking, too, of the future with bright, hopeful hearts. Presently a silence crept over us all—you know it does sometimes, though you can't tell why—and in that silence we could hear distinctly a rustling sound just under the window. What was it? "Nothing." Of course that was what most of the party tried to think. Then some one suggested "the wind," although it was a still night, cold and clear and frosty, not wind enough to stir a leaf in one of the bushes. Tired of waiting for Aunt Bess to go on with a tale she was telling, we begged her to proceed, but scarcely had she taken up the thread of it than my mother started to her feet, exclaiming:

"It *is* the yellow holly!—I thought so," and away she sped to the hall-door, followed by our father and as many of the party as could be won from the warm fireside by curiosity.

I remember that I made my way to mamma's

side—oh, what a rebuke would have been mine at any other time for coming out into the chill night air!—and stood on the steps staring out into the darkness, in which nothing was visible but the dim shapes of trees and evergreens.

"My dear, what does all this mean?" inquired my father, who was wholly puzzled by his usually quiet wife's impetuous proceeding. "There is no one here, and nothing to be seen."

Our mother hesitated, and drew a deep sigh.

"I am sure there *was* something," she answered. "I could not be mistaken. Some one was trying to cut down the yellow holly."

Every one spoke at once. My father said something about her having "yellow holly on the brain," which I thought must be most uncomfortable. Aunt Bess murmured, "Nonsense," while Aunt Lucy said outright, "It was all fancy." Then every one of them went back, shrugging their shoulders, to the fire, and only I and my mother remained unconvinced upon the broad stone steps.

"They may say what they like, Lola," she said (Lola was a sort of pet name which I don't know how I came by), "I am perfectly certain that some one *has* been here, and very likely is lurking behind the bushes now till we disappear."

"But, mamma, what does any one want with our holly?"

"To sell, Lola. It would fetch a good price if it were sold at Christmas-time. Yellow holly is always scarce;" and then we, too, went back to the dining-room party, both of us cold and both of us somewhat restless.

Aunt Bess had got on with her tale so far that perhaps my interest was lost, or perhaps it was only that, do what I would, my attention wandered out into the cold and darkness—to the yellow holly.

Could any one, indeed, want the glossy leaves and bright berries so much as to come and cut at the bush by stealth? My ideas of right and wrong were well defined, and my experience of human nature so limited that I could not imagine such iniquity possible; at any rate, if possible, some great, terrible need must be pressing upon the guilty person. Was somebody very poor and very hungry, with perhaps a number of little children crying for food—unhappy little children who had no hope of a Christmas dinner and presents? Some such vision passed before my small imagination and worked so powerfully upon it that, in spite of all my efforts, I gave vent to a low deep sob, which broke up the tale Aunt Bess was bringing to a close and drew the eyes of all the party upon my poor little self.

What was it? was I ill, or unhappy, or frightened? these and many more were the questions showered on me, but I responded to none of them. I just grasped the terrible truth that Charlie—my best-loved brother—had called me "a muff," and under the weight of that blow I collapsed and hid my face in the folds of my mother's dress, sobbing out something unintelligible about "yellow holly."

"I can't think what possesses the child," exclaimed my father rather impatiently. "Let us by all means clear up the mystery of the holly bush, and then perhaps there will be peace."

I clearly remember that though I was sorry he seemed vexed, my sorrow was tempered with the pleasure of knowing that a search was to be made. *Supposing* my visionary imagination had suggested the truth, I was sure my parents would pardon the thief and supply the wherewithal to procure a Christmas dinner for the hungry children I pictured so clearly.

This time, my father headed the procession to the front door, lantern in hand, and with a look upon his face which I understood to mean that he was not going to be trifled with Charlie was by his side, I clinging to my mother's hand with strangely combined sensations of pleasure and fear, while the aunts, uncles and cousins followed, all now eager to investigate the business.

Raising high the lantern in search of the intruder, if intruder there might be, my father's quick eyes caught sight of the holly tree, glorious no longer, but decapitated!—its berried top cut off and carried away doubtless between the period of our first alarm and the present search.

Surprise, indignation, regret—these were the different sentiments expressed by the company; but I was speechless under the blow which had fallen upon my fancied scene. No discovered thief imploring pardon, no special pleading on my own part, which I had decided upon as a means of melting the paternal heart, no charming *finale* of Christmas beef and even pudding carried to bright-eyed hungry children in some poor garret—only the fine holly ruthlessly hacked about and damaged for many a year to come, and its glory carried away.

Next day the story formed the staple of conversation at dinner, where more relations arrived to keep Christmas with us; but the mystery remained such, nor did any one expect it would ever be cleared up.

It was February, piercing weather, the ground covered with deep snow, and more snow falling. It was a hard time for the poor—hard even in our part of the world, where the very lowest class were far better situated than the average working-folk of London. Our mother instituted soup-making in the kitchen twice weekly for those whose need was greatest, and thus we came to know that the Parkers were in trouble—a somewhat rough, low family who lived down by the river-side, the worst quarter of our region. Cook was despatched to visit them with a basket of such articles as my mother deemed useful in illness, but she came back to say it was Parker himself who was ailing, and he would touch nothing that was sent—only turn his face to the wall and say "he'd rather be let alone."

"I will go myself to the house," said our mother, and she went, but only with the same result; Parker grumbled out his desire for "gentlefolks not to come prying and poking into *his* place."

"He don't mean one half of it, mum," said poor Mrs. Parker, following my mother to the door, with her apron at her eyes and countless apologies upon her lips. "He's that ill it's my belief he don't rightly know what he's a-saying of, or he'd be grateful for your kindness, mum."

After that for several weeks, baskets of food were sent down at regular intervals for the sick man, but the news which was brought back was only that he grew worse rather than better, and seemed as averse as ever to receive any help, although his wife made up for *that* deficiency. At last came a day when the eldest Parker boy arrived at the kitchen entrance crying bitterly, and begging for "the lady to come and see father, who was dying."

Without a moment's hesitation, my mother made herself ready and went out into the cold with little ragged Bob by her side, while I sat dreaming over my lesson-books—dreaming of this strange terrible death, which in spite of all I had been told never did seem to me *real*. I was a thoughtful child, and I must have been turning over this subject in my mind for an hour or more, trying to make out how it would feel to be dying, trying to imagine what it would be when one *was* dead, trying in my childish way to discover some of those things which God has kept hidden from us in love and mercy until in heaven they are all made bright and clear. Suddenly my mother laid her hand on my head, and as I started up I saw tears standing in her eyes.

"He is dead, my little girl," she said, and her voice seemed low and almost sad. "Poor Parker was dying when I got there, and I stayed to the end."

I said nothing, but all the puzzled dreaming and wondering came over me still more strongly and I glanced curiously at my mother who had come from the very presence of this terrible death.

"Who do you think cut down our holly?" said mamma, much to my surprise, for I had almost forgotten the events of Christmas Eve.

"I don't know, mamma—I was thinking about Parker."

"So was I, Lola. It was poor Parker's doing, and he sent for me that he might tell me so. It was because of this he could not bear to take help from this house, nor would he I think have received it at all but for his wife and children. He was in great distress at Christmas-time, and as he passed here almost daily the thought came into his mind of making money by the sale of evergreens, and those he could easily steal. For several nights he had come and cut from our bushes, but the yellow holly he had left to the very last—to Christmas Eve."

"Was he sorry, mamma, that he wanted to tell you this?"

"Sorry for that and for all the sins of his life, my child. So sorry, that he was quite willing to let me tell him of the life and death of Christ —the pouring out of His Blood upon the Cross that we might every one be cleansed from our sins."

It seemed very still and very solemn there in the bright warm library, with mamma's face looking so pale and strange—I could not bear the silence.

"Oh, mamma, you are not angry with poor Parker? I dare say he was very hungry and did not know what to do;" but as I said it I felt that there was no shadow of anger in my mother's heart as she thought of the dead man.

Perhaps she did not hear what I had said. I do not know, for I never liked to ask her. But she seemed as if she had forgotten all about me just then, and there was a far-away look in her eyes which only came sometimes when she felt very sad or grave.

"Ah, little Lola," she said at last, getting up from her seat by the fire, "let us ask God to give us the same repentance for our many sins against Him, and the same trust in the dear Saviour which has been given to this poor ignorant man."

She went away to her room then, and I knew she would not want me to follow her; but there by myself I knelt down and said a little prayer to God, and always since those days the sight of yellow holly has brought to my mind the remembrance of poor Parker and his repentance.

The One Ghost of my Life.

GHOST! does the word make you shiver and feel funny all over? I know that is the effect on some small people; yes, and larger ones too, who ought, of course, to know better than be even the very least bit afraid. Sometimes I wonder how it is that however careful mammas may be, however strict about what tales are told and what books are read, every little boy and girl seems to get to know there is some mysterious talk about ghosts, and *some few* get to believe in it too, which is a great pity.

Now I never was sent to school, so I heard no ghost stories that way, nor, indeed, in any other; for up to the present time, when

I have been "grown-up" so long, I don't believe I ever heard a "downright good ghost story," as boys say. Still the word was familiar in some degree, and, moreover, I had a sort of understanding that it meant something very terrible, which must be spoken of in whispers; and then Charlie (when he came home from his "Academy" at Brighton) used to say that it was "a ghost," whenever there was a sound in the house which we did not quite know the cause of, especially if such sounds came to our ears in the dusky evening time.

Now then for my story, after trying to explain just what I understood of this terrible subject.

It was autumn—the dreary, wild weather which comes after summer has quite gone—when the trees are bare and the wind sighs and moans round the house, or rises to a wild sort of shriek on stormy nights. I expect this same wind gets the name of "ghost" without deserving it. He is such a noiseless and yet such a noisy fellow; he wails and cries, and enters doors and windows, and blows out candles, and parts curtains, yet never a hand, or foot, or figure has he to help in the business.

Yes, believe me, Mr. Wind is the true name of the hero of many popular ghost stories, and if you are as sensible as I hope, you will try and find the culprit out. But yet he wasn't *my* ghost—the one and only ghost who ever managed to frighten me all my life long.

I must come back to my first point and say " it was an autumn night," upon which *Somebody* begs me to " get on," even though she is all in a quiver, partly from fear and partly from curiosity.

I was alone and in bed—worse than all, my parents were out for the evening, my brother at school, the servants down in the kitchen at supper, and my own small self the only occupant of the upper regions of the house.

I was in the dark too—fancy that! But then I must tell you it had always been my choice. We had not taken to have gas in the bedrooms in those days, and if there was one thing I disliked more than another it was a night-light. For one thing, it made the room so shadowy and dim; for another, I could not help watching to see how it was getting on—whether it meant to be "awkward," as nurse termed it, and go out with a fizz and splutter, or whether its paper meant to catch light and startle me with a tremendous blaze, ending in sudden darkness. On the whole I distrusted night-lights then as I do now, and I would have none of them.

So there I lay, feeling lonely, though not as yet *frightened*, wishing very much that mamma did not go out to parties, or that *I* could go out to parties, and passing on to the consideration of what lovely dresses I would wear when I *did* go out to parties, until I had succeeded in making myself very thoroughly awake.

Nurse used to tell me that if I thought of running water, or tried to count a flock of sheep, I should get to sleep directly, but it never proved a success to *me*, and on the present occasion I was not disposed from past experience to try the remedy for my open-eyed wakefulness. I am not quite sure that I did not rather prefer lying awake, so that I should see mamma when she came to my bedside, as she always did before she went to her own room each night. Still, if I had only known how frightened I was going to be, I am sure I should have counted sheep or anything else as a means of closing my eyes.

It is not easy to keep count of time when you are in the dark and there isn't a clock within hearing; but it seemed as if I had been in bed hours and hours when suddenly a feeling came over me that I was not by myself. Do you know what I mean? The sort of feeling if you go upstairs in the dark and meet one of your sisters on the landing, and, without hearing or seeing her, you understand there is some one there and say, "Is it you?"

Well, that was how I felt that night in bed, when I had been listening to the wind and the rain, and everything else there was to listen to —even the laughter at the kitchen supper-table, which seemed a very long way off.

Now I knew that the wind could *sigh*— hadn't it been "sighing" all the evening in the leafless trees which grew close to my bedroom window?—but it never did and never will give a sigh like *something* did quite near to me, at the very foot of my bed in fact. I don't think I was a very nervous child in the usual way, but upon that occasion I could feel my heart beating " twenty-four to the dozen," as folks say. Though I should like to have demanded " Who is there ?" in majestic and awe-striking tones, my voice seemed gone away, and I simply pulled the bed-covering over my head, at the risk of suffocation, and trembled exceedingly. Next thing there was a very decided yet faint rustling sound, which brought to my mind Charlie's reference of all such mysterious noises to " ghosts "—this must be a ghost come to visit me in my solitude!

It was a terrible thought, and I began to review the shortcomings of the day : had I done something so bad as to merit a ghostly warning ? But no, I remembered that mamma had commended me for being a very good child just before she went out, and since then I knew I had been more than ordinarily obedient and amiable, to nurse, in the hope of sitting up somewhat later, instead of being hurried to "the best place for naughty, troublesome children." A few more minutes — which seemed hours—of silence, during which I tried to reason with myself, and to decide that it was very silly and very wicked to be afraid, and that there was nothing in my room, nothing and no one but the usual furniture and myself.

All this I honestly tried to be convinced of; but then came a fresh sound, one unmistakably real and near—a "jinking," clanking sort of noise, though faint, much as a chain or a bunch of keys would make if you moved it with your foot along the floor.

Once more I thought of demanding "Who is there?" and once more I failed to articulate one single word. I grew cold, I grew hot, I felt thirsty, I felt sick; my teeth chattered and yet the perspiration stood upon my forehead (well it might under the weight of the bedclothes).

I suppose that all these sensations and thoughts and fears could not really have occupied more than perhaps half an hour at the very most, yet it seemed to me as if the night must have nearly passed since nurse went downstairs, and I wondered greatly why I had not heard her return, and why papa and mamma were so very late coming home. All was silent then in the room; I began to peep over the coverings which I had drawn around me and take a little fresh air. The ghost had perhaps intended his visit for some one else, and, finding his mistake, had quitted the apartment.

Vain hope! That moment I could feel distinctly that the bed-clothes were being moved by some strong yet stealthy power. Fancy!— it was no fancy, I can tell you: they were going, going, going; but before it came to "gone" I had found voice enough to give one long piercing shriek, sufficient to rouse the household even had they been sleeping. The next thing I knew was that there was a loud ring at the hall-door, a sound of many voices and hurried footsteps, and then, oh joy! not nurse only, but papa and mamma (to say nothing of cook and the housemaid in the background) were in my room.

"It's the nightmare," said papa, while my mother bent over me and tried to soothe me after what she believed to have been some horrible dream. In vain I sobbed, "It was a

ghost, a real dreadful ghost;" they told me
that such things could not be, that the spirits
of the blessed were with God in heaven, and
the spirits of the lost could never come from
their terrible place to frighten children. Still
I was unconvinced, for I knew I had not slept,
and so it could have been no dream and no
nightmare which had startled me. "Some one
has been here, some one who gave such great
sighs, and the clothes *did* move; they slipped
and slipped though I lay so still—oh, mamma,
it must have been a ghost, please look everywhere." Such was my appeal, and my parents,
seeking to cure my fears for once and all, set to
work "ghost-hunting," as they said. In the
wardrobe—no one to be seen; behind the window curtains; under the bed—ah! there was
my ghost hiding away so quietly. It wasn't
white, as of course ghosts ought to be, but
black as coal, and it gave a whine which never
could have come from any ghostly voice, one
which made me laugh till the tears ran down
my face. For that great black form which
came out from its lurking-place was nothing
more nor less than dear old Nep, our house-

dog, who finding it lonely no doubt had managed to free himself from the foot of the kitchen stairs where he was fastened at night, and had come softly up to my room with a quiet footstep, hoping I dare say to remain there till morning.

I expect he was stretching himself out for a nap with a deep sigh of satisfaction when first I became aware of his presence, and that his chain rattled a little in his movements; and possibly Master Nep thought it was not fair for me to have all the warm wrappings, and so he tried to paw them gently off the bed. Poor ghost! he was led off looking as if he blamed me for his discovery, while I composed myself for a good night's rest after the happy clearing out of such a great mystery. That was the last time I ever accused a ghost of disturbing me at night, and if I chance to hear any strange sounds I try to find out their real cause, which always is something very commonplace. You do the same, little people, who read my story, and take my word for it that you will always find it the way to cure yourselves of foolish fears; and, better than all, remember that in the very darkest night you are watched by the great, good God Who can and will keep all harm from coming near you, and Who "gives His angels charge" over every one of us.

Dollie and I.

"DOLLIE" was my friend. Her real name was Dorothea, but no one called her so, I suppose, because it was such a long stiff-sounding word not suited at all to such a merry little girl. It suited some one else far better, and that was Dollie's aunt, who sometimes came to stay at the Hill House. Oh how frightened I was when I had been spending an afternoon there, and we were sent for to go down into the drawing-room. The half-hour seemed more like a half day when Miss Dorothea Neville sat in the high-backed chair which seemed to be the one seat she liked. It was not because she was unkind —oh no, she never was that, but somehow the sharp glance of her eyes made me uncomfortable, and her tales of "when *I* was a child" convinced me that neither I nor Dollie could ever come up to her ideas of what was pretty and proper in little ladies.

We used to have very happy times at the Hill House. I never could quite decide whether I liked the garden and the fruit, the swing, the summer-house and the hayfield in summer, or the games at hide-and-seek on winter days, when we found such wonderfully secret places in some of the nooks and corners of the old-fashioned rooms and passages. To be sure, I often felt half afraid of the big dark pictures on the walls; the ladies in their ruffles and the gentlemen with funny hats did look so *very* much disposed to come out of their heavy frames and scold us children who romped and laughed so much more than I suppose *they* were ever allowed to do in their young days. I know I felt as if the worst of their displeasure would be vented upon me, because I was encouraging Dollie to be so very different to stately Nevilles of former times.

Still, in spite of my fears, those were happy

visits, especially now I look back upon them through the shadows of so many years.

I was going to tell you of how Dollie and I amused ourselves, but her aunt Dorothea's name has recalled to my mind something which brought us into trouble — all through her too!

Mrs. Neville had several trunks full of old dresses which had belonged in former days to the ladies of the Hill House, and Dollie had told me how lovely they were, how stiff and rich the brocades, how dainty the high-heeled shoes, and best of all she had promised that "some-day" she would coax her mamma to shew them to me.

If ever we had a little tiff (you know that even if you love your favourite friend ever so much, such a thing *will* happen now and then), Dollie would say, "Very well—I shan't ask mamma to shew you the dresses in the big trunks," and this threat often brought about a reconciliation. If we felt inclined to sit and "suppose" things in the twilight hour, we generally tried to fancy ourselves dressed up in some of the flowing trains and wonderful head-dresses which were concealed in the "big trunks," and when we hid in the lumber-room we generally chose to crouch behind those same "big trunks" with a feeling of reverence and almost of awe—at any rate I know *I* did.

Only once in the eleven years of her life had Dollie seen inside them—the day when Harold, her baby-brother, had been christened, and she was allowed to go with nurse to put away the old lace cap and robe in which he, and so many Nevilles before him, had been attired for the occasion. It had been only a glimpse—just a peep at a few silks and satins which lay uppermost, but the memory of what she saw was stamped upon Dollie's mind for ever, and one delicate pea-green satin was the one in which she desired to see herself arrayed if ever the opportunity came, while I—the dark-eyed and dark-haired—should sport an amber and white brocade.

One dull November day as I looked out of the dining-room at home, wishing very much that there were no such things as lessons, I saw nurse from the Hill House coming up the drive; and when I heard that she was asking to speak to mamma I scented an unlooked-for invitation. "Mrs. Neville had gone away for two or three days, and Miss Dollie felt dull all alone with her aunt"—that was the excuse for asking for my presence, not for the day only, but for the two days and two nights which must pass before my little friend's mamma came home.

I was wild with delight. Truly I was not fond of leaving my home, but then, to be with Dollie was a great pleasure, and there was something dignified and grown-up in announcing to the household that I was off to Hill House for " a few days."

It did not take long to get me ready. My every-day merino frock was quite nice enough for anything—so said Dollie's nurse; all I could need beside was a silk to put on in the evening when I went down to the drawing-room.

At those words I half repented that I had begged to accept the invitation. Till then I had forgotten all about Miss Dorothea, who was making one of her long stays with her brother. How very terrible it would be to spend half an hour in that grave presence, with those sharp eyes noting every tone and gesture, and no gentle Mrs. Neville to make it easier for us children, and find us some game which helped to divert our minds from the thought of the severe-looking face which seemed always turned towards us.

I could not for very shame whisper to mamma that I would " rather stay at home," but I know I felt more than half inclined to cry when I bade her good-bye, and heard her say that Thomas should bring a little box over to me in less than an hour, containing all I should need for my short visit.

A great lump came in my throat as I descended the hall-steps, and my eyes filled with tears, but I concealed it all with an attempt at coughing, which set nurse "wondering" if I should take cold being out on such a damp, raw day.

But when Dollie's face was visible above the blind of one of the upper windows, and when she ran into my arms and declared herself so happy, "so very happy," I forgot my fears and anxieties, or rather I cheered myself with reflecting that it was still early, and that a great many hours must pass before the dreaded visit to the drawing-room and Miss Dorothea. We had a charming day, for Dollie's nurse was in the very best and sweetest of tempers.

First of all we dressed the dolls in their smartest clothes, and, after seating them in chairs, left them to smile vacantly there all day. Then we did some bead-work, but Dollie said it made her neck ache to stoop so, and we both agreed that picking up beads was "stupid." We next rambled about in the long passages upstairs, "supposing;" and paid a visit to the lumber-room and the big trunks, sighing as we wondered if the long hoped-for day would ever arrive when we should feast our eyes upon their contents.

As we sat there talking, nurse's voice and a bell ringing violently reminded us of dinner, and we descended in all haste to the nursery.

In Mrs. Neville's absence Dollie was to take her meals with Rosy and Harold; but though we were disposed to look down with some contempt upon the "little ones," we greatly preferred their company to that of Miss Neville, so there was no complaining.

Dollie had confided to me that she had a "plan" for the afternoon, but in spite of all my entreaties she kept her secret, and, when I saw a great whispering going on between her and nurse, I felt disposed to be "huffed" at her want of trust in me.

"It's toffee-making!" she cried, after winning an evidently reluctant assent. Oh charming tidings! I felt no longer aggrieved, but accompanied Dollie to the kitchen with a light heart and lighter steps to persuade the cook to bestow the necessary ingredients.

Butter, sugar, treacle. We set them down triumphantly on the nursery-table and gazed with rapture at the sight.

"If you are going to make as much toffee as *that*, young ladies," said nurse with dignity, "we shall have you both sick before you go to bed."

She looked very much like depriving us of a portion of our spoils, only we began coaxing her so much. We danced round her, we said she was a darling, an angel, a love of an old nursey; we promised not to be sick; we undertook to eat ever so much bread-and-butter at tea-time, and in the end gained our point, for the fire was arranged and an earthenware pipkin set upon it containing the good things which were to result in toffee.

Dollie was head-cook, burning her face terribly over the fire as she stirred up the boiling mixture with a wooden spoon. I gave my attention to the making and buttering of little shallow paper dishes in which the contents of the pipkin were to be poured at the proper crisis, Rosy and Harold watching with widely-opened and admiring eyes.

A slight shriek from Dollie—great excitement amongst the nursery party. Was the toffee burning? What was amiss? "Burnt her tongue" as she tasted a little out of the spoon. That was all, and a great weight was taken from my mind, though, as I said these words, Dollie echoed, "All!" somewhat reproachfully, adding, "you wouldn't like it if it was you!"

At length the operation was completed, the little papers were full, and Dollie and I put the tips of our fingers into the quickly-cooling toffee which remained in the spoon, and pronounced it "delicious."

We next retired to wash our hands and faces, which nurse suggested as a necessity; and by the time that was done we found the contents of the paper dishes quite eatable, and despised the idea of it being far better to wait till the toffee was perfectly cold.

Perhaps I should shock you if I owned how much we consumed—of course the little ones and nurse had some though. However, Dollie confided to me that she began to feel "the least bit in the world sick," and it was then we decided that we did not care so very very much for toffee and would give the remainder to the servants in the kitchen.

After the excitement of cooking every amusement seemed flat and dull, and we hung discontentedly about the nursery, complaining of "nothing to do." We were on the very verge of quarrelling from sheer want of occupation when a bright idea entered Dollie's busy brain: she hastened to whisper it to me this time, not to nurse.

ing a candle she proceeded to investigate the matter, accompanied by one of the servants.

It is needless to describe our dismay, or aunt Dorothea's displeasure. Dusky as the light was growing, I was immediately sent home in disgrace, while Dollie was sentenced to the nursery until her mamma came back.

Mrs. Neville was not hard of heart when we explained the circumstances which took us into the lumber-room, but she told us it was another instance of the mischief which Satan is supposed to find for "idle hands to do." I think the feeling of shame in Miss Dorothea's presence was sufficient punishment, and one which lasted many a long day; besides, neither Dollie nor I were ever allowed any more hide and seek in the vicinity of the discovered treasures, and nurse kept a sharp watch over our comings and goings. I think it cured us of curiosity and meddling, though we always felt that it was Miss Dorothea's fear of thieves which had got us into trouble, and anticipated the confession we had purposed making to Dollie's mamma.

"Housekeeping Troubles."

YES, "housekeeping troubles." I had tasted their bitterness, had felt their burden before I was quite twelve years old.

I was the mother of a family, a large family of doll-children, and naturally I took an interest in getting them suitable food. But, oh what difficulties I encountered! Since my grown-up days, I have known what it was to be located in a little village where there was but one butcher's shop, and on certain days nothing to be had from it, and it brought to my mind childish sensations when I believed my dolls were hungry, and I had next to nothing to set before them.

Sometimes my pocket-money, and therefore sweets, ran short; at other times cook was hard of heart, and would give me nothing out of the pantry, and even mamma objected to the quantity of biscuits which disappeared, and therefore stopped the supplies.

All these came under the heading of house-keeping troubles, but it is of the difficulties of one special day of which I am going to tell.

I had a cousin staying with me—my cousin Belle. She was older than myself, yet we played together and were very good friends. One of our favourite games was, that we were ladies of fashion paying morning-calls and exchanging visits. We prepared cards to leave at each other's houses. On mine was written the name of "The Hon. Mrs. Skeggs," on Belle's there was inscribed, in a neat round hand, the title of " Lady Seraphina Mortimer," so you see she was decidedly the more aristocratic of the two.

The Lady Seraphina had graciously accepted an invitation to spend "a long day" with her friend Mrs. Skeggs.

"Come early, dear, as early as you possibly

"*Housekeeping Troubles.*" 47

can," I had said when the matter was arranged; yet like other ladies I found it embarrassing to be understood literally, and to be frightened by a loud rat-tat-tat before I had arranged my toilette. I must explain that I had risen early and begun the dressing of my children before breakfast. Directly I was allowed to leave the table, I arranged my reception-room with great taste, and with so much depending upon one pair of hands don't you think it was *rather* inconsiderate of Lady Seraphina to arrive at nine o'clock? the hour was just striking!

My hair was rough, my hands not of the whitest, my cooking preparations incomplete, and there was Lady Seraphina smiling calmly from beneath the shade of a parasol she had borrowed from mamma's closet on the stairs, and with a long black silk skirt Aunt Bess had allowed her to put on for the occasion.

Of course I said "I was delighted to see her," "not at all too early," "quite charmed," and all the other polite things I could think of; but no sooner was she divested of her walking costume and fanning herself comfortably as she lounged upon the sofa, than I made an excuse to get away. The children! really nurse was so long in bringing them downstairs that if she would pardon me, I must go and see what was the matter.

Lady Seraphina bowed her assent most graciously, while I ran upstairs feeling as much vexed as any other "Mrs. Skeggs" would have done that my guest had arrived so unreasonably early.

My bedroom was pantry for the occasion—pantry and kitchen combined. Kneeling on a chair at the chest of drawers, I prepared two dishes of almonds and raisins, cut up and sugared an orange, concocted a "trifle" out of some jam, milk, and grated biscuits, which I hoped would taste better than it looked. I had a square of hard-bake also, an ounce of pear-drops, and a halfpenny stick of chocolate to make up the feast, which I surveyed with great satisfaction when my arrangements were complete.

Back then to my guest, after hastily slipping on a muslin skirt which trailed on the ground, and hiding the misfit of the body with a black lace shawl, all borrowed, for the day, like Lady Seraphina's finery.

She was fidgetting about the room when I went in, and seemed rather cross, but we began talking about the weather and the servants for a bit, until we grew tired of personating such grand ladies, and became our own real selves once more.

Being free from the restraints of high breeding, we each declared we were very hungry, and Belle assisted me in carrying in the repast. Unfortunately I upset a little of the trifle on the stairs, but we spooned it up carefully and rubbed the carpet with a clean pocket-handkerchief, and Belle comforted me with the assurance that it would taste none the worse for the accident.

We spread our table and then retired to bring down the children, but as some of the sashes had to be changed to suit Belle's taste, and Maud's white muslin replaced by her crimson merino, it took some time—sufficient time for mischief to be done in our banqueting room.

What should *you* feel if you had a Lady

Seraphina Mortimer to spend the day, and after preparing a suitable dinner for such a distinguished guest, found the table cleared just at the moment when she confessed herself "starving?"

I was fond, devotedly fond, of our little dog Rough, but when I saw him give the finishing "lick" to the dish of trifle, and noted the famine he had created, I was nearer inflicting punishment on him than ever I had been before. You will admit that I had received great provocation, and there was some excuse for the tears I shed, which were only dried by a liberal contribution from mamma's store-room to make up for the disappointment. Belle and I soon dished up another meal for ourselves and family, and thus happily, for that day, ended my housekeeping troubles.

On an Island.

WE once had an adventure, I and my brother Charlie. It was in midsummer holidays when the days were warm and long and half our time was spent out of doors, either under the shady trees, or in the summer-house, or in the hayfield; anywhere which promised a shelter from the hot rays of the sun.

From our garden we could look down on the river—the pretty winding river Lea; and Charlie was wild after boating. He used to spend whole mornings in this way with one or two of his friends also home for the holidays, but I never was fortunate enough to get leave to be of the party, and my "rows" were few and far between, because they only came when papa had a leisure evening.

One day, however, Charlie confided to me that he meant to take me on the river; the two Marshalls were off to Richmond, and he was ready to fall back upon my society as nothing better offered.

It never occurred to him to ask leave. As for me, I dismissed the thought lest—if acted upon—it might bring disappointment, and I sought to calm any disturbance of conscience by reflecting that mamma had only forbidden me to go boating with the other boys.

Charlie suggested that as we should not be back for lunch, it would be the wisest plan to take some refreshments with us, and I was despatched to persuade cook to put us up a little supply. Alas! she was not there, the kitchen seemed deserted except by the grey parrot who screamed "get along" at the top of his voice, and then I remembered that cook had gone herself down to the fruit garden to see the condition and quantity of the currants and raspberries which she wanted for preserving.

What was I to do? Charlie had said "make haste," and I always did what he told me, besides, I was in mortal fear that if I kept him long he would depart without me.

Quietly I peeped into the larder—oh! how that dreadful parrot did shriek—and looked round. Snatching up a small basket which hung conveniently there, I put into it, with eager trembling fingers, a small fruit pie, half a loaf, and a substantial piece of cheese, and hurried away as I had come, to be scolded vigorously by Charlie for being "such a time."

I am glad to say I had the grace to feel a little ashamed of myself as we passed round by the library window, and I saw the back of mamma's head. Of course she believed we were all right, for we were of an age to be trusted, yet how mean, how unworthy of that trust did I feel myself as I went out at the back entrance by Charlie's side, and so into the lane which led down to the river.

Once there, however, my spirits rose. It was a splendid day, and the water sparkled brightly in the sunshine, yet a pleasant breeze waved the branches of the trees and cooled my burning cheeks. There were one or two little islets in that part of the river, and Charlie proposed we should land upon one of these and eat our lunch. We did so, and surely never did currant tart and bread and cheese taste so good, and never had we felt so hungry as we did that bright July morning.

We had turned our backs upon the boat, and I was gazing dreamily at the blue sky through a network of leaves while Charlie was launching out into some of his fine schemes for the future. He was going to be a sailor, so he said in those days, and he should bring me home birds and shells and beautiful shawls, gold dust, copper ore, and everything else, either useful or ornamental, which he had ever heard of. Suddenly there fell upon our ears the "plash" of a boat in the water, and starting to our feet we found that we were captives on our island, while a hoarse rude laugh showed that some of the rough "ferry" boys had played this trick upon us.

I was ready to cry, but Charlie bade me so sternly not to do so that I choked back my tears and pocketed my handkerchief. He

represented to me that it was not as if we were
in some deserted spot. True, the boating on the
river was but small during the morning hours,
but even if no one passed by till evening we
were certain to be picked up then; meanwhile,
we had not finished all the currant tart, to say
nothing of bread and cheese.

How long that day seemed, yet no one came
down the river as far as the island. I stood
gazing up towards the ferry, hoping to discern
some distant speck which should turn into a
boat in due time, but in vain. Then I thought
of the search which would be made for us, how
our names would echo in the garden walks,
how alarmed our mother would be, and then,
worse than all, she would feel no more trust in
such naughty runaway children.

I could never tell you the good resolutions
which I made on that little island, how I
promised God that if He would only send
some one to find us I would never, never do
anything disobedient or wilful any more.

As for Charlie, he paced up and down on the
small bit of grass like a caged lion, feeling very
uncomfortable, I know, by a look which always

came on his face when his mind was ill at ease.
He was very good to me though, for when he
proposed to swim across to the bank and so
get another boat to take me home, I cried out
in such terror at being left, and such fear of
his being drowned, that he gave up the idea,
although he *did* call me "a little idiot."
There was a look in the sunshine and in the
shadows which told me it was just five o'clock,
when we saw a boat coming down the river
with two men rowing and a party of ladies
and children evidently going some excursion.
Charlie hailed them, and upon hearing our
case they kindly turned about and took us to
our starting point close by our own home.
Ah, how ashamed were the two faces which
went in at the gate and round the high-grown
laurel walk which was the back way to the
house; I thought at the time that just in such
a guilty shamefaced way must Adam and Eve
have looked at each other after they had eaten
the forbidden fruit! We were not scolded or
punished perhaps as some children would have
been, but the very worst of *all* our punishments fell upon us, and that was the loss of

our mother's trust for the rest of that holiday. Charlie was prohibited from any boating, while I was not suffered even to play in the garden without a servant's eye upon me. I can tell you I bitterly regretted my visit to the river island, but I did try to keep the resolution I made during my day's captivity, and when at last mamma said "yes" to my often-repeated question, "Can't you trust me yet?" I felt happier than I could ever tell you.

Berengaria.

HAVE you ever been to Madame Tussaud's Exhibition of Wax-work? If so, perhaps you remember the figure of the pretty Queen Berengaria, of Navarre, by the side of her fierce-looking husband; and this was how I came to think of such a very uncommon name for a new doll.

I must tell you first that I had *won* her, and you know as well as I that anything you win is doubly precious. Perhaps, when I say that Berengaria was the reward of playing my minor scales correctly, some little girl may sympathise with the pleasure I felt when I clasped her in my arms. I never did like playing scales—pretty airs were quite a different matter—but as for *minor* scales, they were simply dreadful!

I used to cry over my music-lessons sometimes, much as I loved music, and all because of these minor scales. At last mamma said that when I knew them perfectly I should have a large wax doll, just such an one as I had long set my heart upon. That promise put fresh spirit into me and also into my fingers, and the very day I could cry "Victory" my beautiful Berengaria was in my possession.

She was blue-eyed like most dolls, but her hair was brown; and I took great pride in this, for all the dolls *I* knew had fair curls or else horrid wiry, black stuff, something like a nigger's.

There was only one trial connected with the arrival of Berengaria—she was not dressed, because mamma thought that the great use of dolls for little girls was that they might learn to sew for them!

I was not expected to make all her clothing — that would have indeed been hard upon Berengaria, for the weather was cold, and a sheet of tissue paper is poor thin covering—

but every afternoon, in what I called "playtime," I was supposed to devote at least an hour to my child's wardrobe.

The first article I chose to try my skill upon was a little flannel petticoat, but I made such a "cobble-stitch" of the herring-boning that I was forced to give it up in despair. Next I tried the skirt of a frock, which fared no better under my inexperienced fingers, and at last I begged mamma to have my doll dressed for me on condition that I really and truly did complete for her a set of pocket-handkerchiefs.

This proposal was agreed to, only it was also agreed that I should still give up my hour to dolls' work, so that I might prepare a set of summer dresses for her by the time they were wanting; and I may as well say here that I kept my promise, and it was the first step to my becoming a very tolerable little needlewoman.

Oh the pride I took in Berengaria!—how delightedly I dressed her in blue merino, and black velveteen, in a flounced silk or evening dress of muslin, or of tarlatane; and all my friends admired and half envied my beautiful doll.

After a while I grew a little tired of dressing and undressing her, and then I made believe she had the fever. Of course this kept her in bed and separated from the rest of my family, and necessitated besides a great deal of messy cookery in my little saucepans. The next thing was to give her change of air, and, as we were not going to the sea-side so soon, I arranged to place my darling in the care of my friend Dollie for a whole long week.

It was silly, I dare say, but Berengaria seemed such a real child to me that I could not part with her without shedding tears; and, wrapping her in a warm cloak, I implored of Dollie to be careful of draughts or any exposure to the cold.

Going to bed that night was sad work, for my doll's empty cradle was there to meet my gaze, and yet I decided that I had parted with her for her good, and reasoned with myself like any other sensible mother. However, I was heartily glad when the week was over and Dollie re-appeared at the appointed hour.

I thought she seemed out of spirits, and after some hesitation the cause was wrung from her. Berengaria had fallen from a high chair, and a deep crack ran across her neck and shoulder, which brought tears to my eyes as I unfastened her wrappings.

I tried to think and say it "didn't matter," for Dollie seemed so very unhappy about it; but my heart was sore, and I bitterly lamented allowing my child to leave me. It really seemed as if that was the beginning of misfortunes for Berengaria, for after that time she was always in the wars, and before her first birthday came round she had grown quite shabby.

I loved her all the same though, perhaps better, because I no longer felt as if she was too good for use. As time went by she lost one of her eyes; but though an undeniable disfigurement, even this affliction had its "bright side," for I was able to feed her through the hole thus provided for the reception of cake, sweets, etc. Once her head came unsewn, and I could not tell you the quantity and variety of undigested food which strewed the carpet—breadcrumbs, bits of biscuit, scraps of cake and such like things which had come into my own possession.

But poor Berengaria came to a sad end after all the love and care I had lavished upon her. It was during one of Charlie's Christmas holiday-times, and the latest amusement he could find for wet days and unoccupied moments was the conveyance of sundry articles from the upper to the lower regions of the house by means of a crane which he had fixed on the top landing of the back staircase. At length he decided that Berengaria must make the descent, remarking, with some truth, that a few bumps and bruises, more or less, would scarcely make any difference in her appearance. I agreed, and ran to the landing-place to receive her into my arms; but, alas for me, and my poor old doll, an unlucky blow against a sharp corner of the staircase split head and neck in two, and it was a corpse, a real, true corpse, which I sat down and cried over, for there was evidently no possibility of reviving her after *this* accident.

We gave her decent burial under a laburnum

tree in the garden, and a little wooden slab was set up to mark the spot, on which was inscribed:

HERE LIES

BERENGARIA,

BELOVED AND LAMENTED

BY

ALL HER FRIENDS.

MY GOLDEN DAYS.

BY

M. F. S.,

AUTHOR OF "CATHERINE HAMILTON," "THE THREE WISHES,"
"STORIES OF THE SAINTS," "CATHERINE GROWN OLDER,"
"FLUFFY," "LEGENDS OF THE SAINTS," "STORIES
OF MARTYR PRIESTS," "TOM'S CRUCIFIX,"
ETC., ETC.

**

London:
R. WASHBOURNE, 18 PATERNOSTER ROW.
1878.

Contents.

Second Series.

	PAGE
"TABLEAUX VIVANTS"	5
"PIETRO"	11
WILLIE'S ESCAPE	19
SEASIDE ADVENTURES	29
THE CAPTAIN'S MONKEY	35
"EIGHTY-EIGHT"	45
A SPRAINED ANKLE	50
DR. SYNTAX	57

MY GOLDEN DAYS.

"Tableaux Vivants."

THE year that my cousin Rosalie spent with us, we seemed to change all our amusements, for she was so much older than I, and even than Charlie, and she knew so many more things to do.

Rosalie's home was in New York. I had an aunt and uncle and seven cousins there whom I had never seen until I was twelve years old, so you may think what a pleasure it was to know that at last some of our American relations were coming to visit us.

There was a great preparation all through the house for days before they were expected to arrive, and I was allowed to superintend the ornamenting of the room which was for Rosalie. By this I mean, that I picked out some nice vases and statuettes for the chimney-piece, made the dressing-table as pretty as it could possibly be, and even took some of my own favourite books for the small shelf which hung against the wall.

I am quite certain that I went twenty times if not more up to a window which commanded a view of the road along which they would have to drive, yet when the carriage *did* draw up I felt so shy and foolish that I would have run away if it had been possible.

Up the steps they came—Aunt Alice, Uncle Phil, and then a tall young lady whom I knew must be my cousin Rosalie. It was a great disappointment to see her so "grown-up," for I never could talk to grown-up people, until I knew them very well; but fortunately Rosalie was not shy at all, and she chatted away so merrily that I forgot I had felt afraid of her, and we became great friends though she was so much the elder.

While uncle and aunt stayed with us there was scarcely anything done but visiting and sight-seeing; however, when they had gone back to New York, leaving Rosalie in England until the following spring, we began to settle down into our usual way of life.

She was not unhappy, this American cousin of ours, when her parents bade her good-bye. There was a little shade upon her face, and her lips quivered as she waved her handkerchief after the departing carriage, but that was all; it was her way to make the best of everything, and a very good way too.

When winter came, Rosalie lamented a great deal for the sleighing to which she had been used in her own gay city, but we did our best for her. Fortunately it was an unusually frosty season, and the ice on our little pond was strong enough for anything; so Charlie, with the help of Tom Marshall, manufactured a sleigh out of an old nursery rocking-chair, in which Rosalie sat like a queen in her fur jacket while they drew her round and round.

But I was going to tell you about the "tableaux vivants," because Rosalie got them up.

We and our friends had been accustomed

to act charades, and had done " Conundrum," "Art-i-choke," and a host more words until we and our audience were tired. As soon as our annual juvenile party was talked of, and we began to discuss what amusements were to be provided, Rosalie suggested the getting-up of these " tableaux."

There was a grand sound about the very name which had a charm for us, but innumerable difficulties cropped up. There must be a regular preparation of dresses, stage, etc., and how could this be managed ?

Rosalie carried her point triumphantly, and proved to mamma that it neither would nor *should* be any " bother " at all. As for the stage, what could be better than the little room leading into the drawing-room, the doors thrown open and curtains hung up. Then for dresses, she would work at them herself if some of the servants could give a little help, and thus the difficulties were settled one by one.

How busy she was to be sure, and yet how merry; it was her bright good-humour which made Rosalie so popular amongst us all.

The first scene was to be composed of two figures only: herself as a Greek slave, dressed in white, which showed off her exquisite fairness to great advantage as she crouched at the feet of her Turkish mistress—dark-eyed Louise Marshall—who was arrayed in mamma's new crimson flannel dressing-gown, and an elaborate turban upon her head.

After this came Charles I. taking leave of his children. Tom Marshall took the character of the poor King, and wonderfully well had Rosalie's nimble fingers managed the dress. Little Fred Renshaw was Duke of Gloucester, and his part would have been perfectly done, only he thought it necessary to give a regular "Boo-hoo" instead of crying decorously and quietly. The part of the Princess Elizabeth was allotted to me, and as I remember an old axiom in the copy-books about "self-praise," I will only say that I enjoyed the situation extremely, and was quite sorry when Charlie rang the bell for the curtain to fall.

The concluding performance was one in which a great many of our young friends took part, and which taxed to its utmost Rosalie's inventive genius. The costume of every European country was represented: a Spanish lady with fan and graceful mantilla, the French peasant-woman with snowy cap, large ear-rings, and wooden sabots, and so forth.

We had many rehearsals, and upon the evening of the party we were much applauded, and "tableaux vivants" became the rage among our circle of young friends for that winter, who voted Rosalie a real treasure.

Long after she had gone back to her home in New York, we thought of all the fun she made for us, and hoped that some day she would stay with us again, but she never did. It seems to me that I was still only a little girl when news came across the Atlantic of Rosalie's marriage, and she had directed her own wedding-cards to me as "Princesss Elizabeth," in memory of the old "tableaux" days.

"Pietro."

IT was summer, and we were at Hastings, and though every one said we should find the heat unbearable, it did not seem any worse than we had left it at home.

Perhaps had we been staying in front of the sea we might have been partially baked, but if you know the terrace of houses just under Castle Hill, you will know too that there we felt every breath of wind there *was* to feel. It was beautiful, too, on summer evenings to sit on the green turf outside the old ruin, looking across seaward at the little quiet waves which came creeping up so softly, or away to the country which stretched upon the other side. We had cut our initials in every available place within the gardens of the castle, we had driven to Fairlight, to Old Roar, to Pett Church, and everywhere else we could think of. We had made up picnic parties to Battle Abbey and Bodiam Castle, driving home in the dusky evening-light when nightingales sang in the hedges and glow-worms glimmered by the road-side; and our pleasant holiday was drawing to a close when we met with poor Pietro.

He had come up the steps to our terrace one evening certainly in each week of our stay, but we had never noticed him or his monkey, which had flourished about in a little red coat, seeking to gain our interest by his funny tricks.

At last, however, a night came when, as we were all seated round the table having a late tea after some pleasant excursion, we heard the miserable organ grinding in such a jerky way that Charlie peeped out between the venetian blinds to see what was going on.

He came back to his bread and butter and shrimps, reporting that "The old fellow seemed precious queer;" and mamma, who still gazed out, said she believed the poor organ-grinder was ill, for he was leaning against the stone parapet as if he felt too exhausted to stand without some support.

It was the old "Partant pour la Syrie" he was playing, when in the middle of the tune there was a sudden pause, and then a muffled sound, half a groan and half a cry.

Papa, Mamma, Uncle Dick, in fact all of us, were out in the space before the terrace in a moment, and so indeed were many more people from the other houses.

The organ-man seemed to have fainted, for he was lying full length upon the pebbly drive, while the monkey clung to him, grinning and chattering defiantly at the crowd which had quickly gathered.

Both Papa and Uncle Dick were tall and strong, and they soon carried the poor fellow across to our house and into the sitting-room on the ground-floor. Mamma poured a teaspoonful of brandy down his throat, and after a few moments it seemed to revive him, for he opened his eyes and looked round him anxiously, and then fell back once more against the cushions we had hurriedly put under his head.

It seemed a long while, though I suppose it was not really many minutes, before Pietro was able to tell mamma in broken French, and an occasional word of English, what his name was, and the street in the old part of the town where he had obtained a lodging for himself, his organ, and monkey.

As soon as he was at all able, poor Pietro seemed anxious to get home, and after he had taken a cup of tea and a little food he started with good-natured Uncle Dick, who insisted on seeing him safely at least part of the way.

We could talk of nothing else for the rest of the evening but the organ-man; wondering what had brought him from his own bright land to our colder climate, wondering too how long his weak-looking frame would bear the hardship and the want which he evidently suffered.

When Uncle Dick came in again he told us

he had been with Pietro to his lodging; a poor almost empty garret in a house situated in one of the poorest streets of old Hastings. He had gained some little knowledge of the Italian's history too, which we heard with the greatest interest.

Like many others of his countrymen, Pietro had come to England believing that it was the way to gain all the wealth and happiness of which he had sometimes dreamed in his little vine-covered cottage. But trouble after trouble had befallen him. First of all his Maddalena died—the good brave wife who had battled against poverty until she could bear it no longer, and putting little Carlo into his father's arms closed her eyes for ever on this world. It was not easy for Pietro to tend the motherless child, and at the same time tramp about to earn a scanty living for them both, but he did his best, and Carlo had ridden contentedly along upon the organ, chattering in baby fashion of all that he saw. Then came his second sorrow—Carlo went to join his dead mother in a land where there is neither want nor sorrow, and Pietro must trudge on alone. That had been all over some three years, during which he had got a monkey to share his labours, and win halfpence from those who would give them, but Pietro himself was growing weak and worn down, and he began to feel that he should never again see his Italian home.

All this Uncle Dick told us, and early next morning Mamma, with Charlie and I, went to the organ-man's lodging. Oh, what a stifling place it was that hot August day! the sun came down with a burning force upon the little attic roof, and poor Pietro, lying on a mattress in the corner, seemed as if he could hardly breathe. The organ stood up against the wall by his side, and the monkey cowered beside it with eyes glittering like diamonds, evidently very angry with us for approaching his master. He could only speak a very few words of English, but by the help of a little French and a little Italian, mamma seemed able to make out what he said. It was this country, this terrible country, which was killing him, so he said—if he could but go back to his own land he should live. Mamma comforted him as best she could with a promise of thinking what could be done to get him home; but she believed that Pietro would never see his sunny Italy again, never even be able to go out with his organ and monkey.

For several days one or other of our parents visited the poor dying man, taking him little dainties to tempt his appetite, and even getting a doctor to go and see what could be done for him. But before the week ended, the woman who kept the house came up to tell us that Pietro was dead: she had gone in to tidy up his room a little, just in time to see him pass away.

Poor organ-man! Only the day before he had begged papa to take "Jacko" if anything happened to him, and for a few days we kept the poor monkey in a temporary cage in our landlady's kitchen. But after that he was sent off to the Zoological Gardens, where I dare say he feels himself very well cared for—much better than in the days when he was carried about on the organ by his old master.

All this is years ago, yet the sight or even the name of Hastings always brings back to my mind the summer holidays when we made acquaintance with poor Pietro.

Willie's Escape.

ONCE upon a time I had a little companion in my lessons and games—Willie, who was the child of some friends mamma had in India, and who stayed with us a few months before he went to school.

When his coming was first talked of, everyone said it would be very "nice" for me; but I had many doubts upon the subject, and thought that perhaps if another lady or gentleman was to go shares in the house and all her pretty things, mamma might not like it any better than *I* liked the idea of having Willie with me.

But when I really saw him, so tiny, so weak and pale, I began to feel inclined to make a great pet of him—only till the next day though, for, once recovered from his journey and quite familiar with us all, Willie played fine pranks. Before dinner-time on the day after his arrival, he had cut his fingers in three places with mamma's penknife, burned a great hole in the schoolroom table-cloth, sent his ball through the staircase window, to say nothing of smaller disasters.

I had promised to be very kind to Willie, but I did feel cross when he persisted in liking his own home so much better than mine. When all was quiet that night, I fancied I heard a strange noise coming from the other side of the corridor, and sitting up in bed I listened. At first it seemed like one of the dogs whining, but after a second or two I knew it came from Willie's room, and throwing on a garden cloak I rushed there.

"Willie, Willie," I began; "don't cry, dear Willie. We all love you, and you will be very happy here, and you shall ride on Bessie every day, and—" but I was cut short by an angry "Get away" from under the bed-clothes.

Deeply hurt, I only paused to remark that I should not have come if he had not been crying, and that in my opinion he was very unkind—very unkind *indeed.*

Upon this expression of my feelings Willie only responded once more, "Get away, *do;*" so I retired with all the dignity I could assume, resolving that should be the very last time I ever got up in the cold to console *anybody.*

Hardly had I curled myself round in my own bed than I caught sight of a small white figure standing in the doorway.

"Are you asleep?" said Willie in a loud whisper.

"No, but I soon shall be," I returned crossly; "what do you want *now?*"

"I was cross just now, and I'm sorry—that's all;" and away he flew, leaving me to reflect upon my own ill-humour. Making many excellent plans for future patience, I fell fast asleep; nor did I wake until it was broad daylight, and I heard Willie's voice shouting "Sally, come up."

Sarah was the maid who had to attend upon him, and when she heard this noise she did "come up," but not in the sweetest temper, for she considered Willie's song a personal insult.

"Now look here, sir," I heard her say; "all this singing and shouting before seven o'clock in the morning won't do."

The only notice Willie seemed to take of the remark was to strike up the second verse of the melody, and from the sounds which came across the landing, I believe he must have been accompanying the song with a dance; at any rate, I was sure from Sarah's next words that she was very near laughing, for she only bade him "lie down one half-hour, and then he should get up."

"You promise?" said Willie doubtfully.

"Yes, sir—at half-past seven to the minute."

"Honour bright?" suggested the small boy.

"Yes, sir, quite bright—though I don't know what you mean, nor did I ever see such a child in all *my* life," murmured Sarah as she retired.

After this there was perfect silence until the big clock on the stairs struck the half-hour. Willie's song burst forth afresh, but

Sarah appeared most promptly, and having dressed him came in to me.

"I beg you won't take pattern by this young gentleman, miss," she said as she curled my hair, and at last pronounced me ready; "I should hope he will soon go to school, before the house is turned upside down."

"Oh, I hope not," I answered, for already I fancied I should miss this odd troublesome little fellow.

But I was going to tell you how Willie once frightened us by running away.

When he joined my daily lessons, I am afraid our governess had a bad time of it, for he was naturally lazy, and I did not work half so well as I had done in former times.

One day—oh, how well I remember it!—such a complaint was made to mamma, that I was sent to my own room, while Willie remained in the play-room.

I felt very cross at first, then sorry; then I only thought how fine the afternoon was, and how very much I should like to go out. With these feelings in my mind I stood gazing from the window, when suddenly I saw a small figure which resembled Willie's steal cautiously across the lawn and vanish in the shade of the tall trees beyond.

Surely mamma had not let him out, keeping me shut up; oh no! she was never unjust. No, it must be that Willie had in some way managed to escape.

How long I stood looking over the garden and wondering what it all meant I could not tell you, but at last I heard the church clock strike four. One hour more and mamma was to come and hear my lessons, and I had not begun them yet! Down I sat on the floor and learned so quickly that it made me more than ever ashamed of myself.

Punctually at five mamma appeared, and I regained my liberty after a very serious little lecture.

In my curiosity I stretched half over the stairs to hear what happened when mamma opened the play-room door, for I was certain Willie was not there. A quick exclamation, my own name called, and I flew downstairs, only too glad of the opportunity of knowing all about it. Ah! what a sight was prepared

for us! Books taken from their shelves and
piled up on the floor to form a ladder by
which the window could be reached; the
curtains pulled down and arranged as the
drapery of a tent made of chairs; old Flora
the spaniel lying within it, a handkerchief
tied like a night-cap round her head, and a
lesson-book under her paws, at which she
was solemnly blinking—all this we saw, but
no Willie; and where could he possibly be?

All I could say was, that I "thought" he
had crossed the lawn as the clock struck four.

Servants were sent in different directions
to seek the truant, yet found no trace of him,
excepting that an old woman living at the turn-
pike some three miles off, said she remembered
a little boy passing who was about young
master's size.

It seemed impossible that Willie should
have wandered so far; however, some one went
that way inquiring at every house and cottage
—in vain.

The sun was sinking below the trees at the
end of the garden, mamma paced the hall
and staircase in misery, while I crept after

her, feeling very frightened and unhappy. Suddenly a bright thought came to Sarah— she would go and look if the child was in the church, she said; and though mamma was doubtful, she continued to protest that it was not an unlikely place to find him in, for that was the day on which it was always open for cleaning purposes.

A long time passed; mamma shook her head at the thought of Sarah's search being successful. Suddenly there was a stir and bustle, for it seemed that the whole household were making for the front door. Following in their train, I beheld Sarah setting Willie down on the steps with a sigh and a good shake.

"Naughty bad boy," she began; but mamma spoiled it all by taking the truant in her arms, while Sarah launched into a long story of how she had been to the verger and made him open the church-door, and after looking everywhere from the belfry to the organ-loft, they discovered Willie cosily asleep in one of the cushioned pews.

"But I *wasn't* comfortable, Sarah," suggested the culprit; "I was ever so hungry before I went asleep, for it's a long while since dinner."

Upon that hint, Willie was given some supper, and sent off to rest without any more questioning.

He told us next day that he had never thought of running away. First of all he learned his lessons, and then made up games until he was tired of them; and at length he resolved to get out of the window and take a walk, returning before he was missed, which he knew would be at five o'clock.

As he passed the old church, the door was open, and in went Willie, looking at all the old tablets on the wall, walking up into the pulpit, and in and out of the square pews, always careful to keep out of sight of the two old women who were sweeping and scrubbing.

At last, feeling tired, Willie went to sit down and rest, and "it was lovely," he said. "The sun shone through the windows, and there was a light over everything—all blue and red and orange; and it made me think about mamma in India, and then about heaven, and I was so happy I forgot about coming home for a long time, and then I went to every one of the doors and they were fastened."

"Were you frightened, Willie—did you cry?" I asked.

Willie hesitated.

"No—I didn't exactly cry, and I wasn't frightened—not *very* I mean. Of course I wanted to get out, and I got so hungry, but I sat down in a pew and I suppose I went to sleep, for I don't remember any more till I felt Sarah shaking me."

I think Willie—and I too—felt rather anxious as to what might be done with him after this escapade; but when mamma found he was really sorry, she gave him a full pardon, only telling him that if he ran away any more he would be sent to school at once. I need only tell you that Willie kept the promise he made then, and when the time came for us to part with him, every one was sorry, even though he had been so troublesome and full of tricks.

Seaside Adventures.

THIS story must come next, because it is about things which happened whilst Willie was still with us.

Glad news came to the schoolroom one day—we were going to the sea, and Charlie was to join us.

I will pass over all the preparations and packing, and only say how delightful it was to feel that the train had really started, and was to take us through tunnels, over bridges, under arches, and miles and miles away to the coast.

For a long time I had been watching for a first glimpse of the waves, when papa suddenly looked up from his paper, and all at once there was a pleasant salt smell, and I cried:

"Look, Willie, look! There's the dear old sea!"

Willie must have been expecting nothing less than stormy sky and big waves, for he looked scornfully at the distant line of bluish-green water.

"It didn't look so when I came from India," he remarked. "It isn't any better here than the duck-pond on Dossington Common—only it's dirtier."

I turned away in speechless disgust; but next day Willie changed his mind, and, as the tide came in, he pronounced it "jolly."

The best part of our time at first was spent on the sands, but at length we grew somewhat weary and wanted a donkey-ride. One day we received permission to go with Sarah to the stand and choose two with the cleanest saddles and best-groomed coats; and thus we started along the parade, meaning to get out into the country.

Sarah walked solemnly enough a few paces behind, and when the donkeys trotted she still managed, by quickening her pace, to keep us in sight. But after a while we struck into a

sort of jerky gallop and left her far away,
evidently nervous and angry, for she was calling and waving her umbrella.

The donkey-boy enjoyed the fun, and with
constant applications of his stick managed to
keep the animals going; but our ride came to
a sudden and calamitous end, for my saddle-girths had never been properly fastened, and
now gave way, so that I and my seat slipped
quietly over the donkey's tail into the dusty
road—none the worse for it excepting from
the fright.

Sarah got up to us then, and nothing would
induce her to let me mount again. In vain I
pleaded; Willie and I were walked home,
hearing all the way that we had had our first
and last ride.

To make up for this trial, mamma promised
us a row on the sea " some day ;" but this day
was so long in coming that Willie and I tried
a little excursion by ourselves, which might
have ended very sadly.

On the beach there were always plenty of
small boats drawn up out of reach of the
waves, and the men who went about in their

shiny hats and blue shirts would ask in the most tantalising way if we wanted a row.

Of course we did — terribly; but were obliged to say, "No, thank you," because our pleasure was always put off till some "tomorrow," which never came.

One day Willie and I had strolled along the beach some distance, grumbling very much at our hard fate, until growing tired we sat down on the shingle close by a nice newly-painted boat, which was drawn up there high and dry. The tide was coming in fast, but we scarcely noticed it, and as Willie talked of the delightful thing it would be to go sailing round the world, away from lessons and from Sarah, we heeded it still less, until one big wave stole up nearly to our toes, and looking round the corner of the rock behind which we had hidden, we saw no chance of getting back.

"Let us get into the boat," cried Willie. "It will only *waggle* a little; we shall be quite safe till the tide goes out. Oh, won't Sarah be in a fume!"

We seated ourselves accordingly, and another wave came up—not angrily and noisily, but swelling all around us so beautifully that we quite enjoyed the motion.

It was not beautiful though a little while after, when we felt certain we were getting out upon the sea, farther from our hiding-place; and, glancing nervously at the shore, we wondered if Sarah would see us, and how we should get back again.

It came out afterwards that we had not been missed from the other groups of children on the beach for some time, and then Sarah's first thought had been to run home and see if we had returned there by ourselves. Finding no trace of us, she rushed back to the sea half-frantic with terror, to see the people crowded together and pointing with frightened faces to some little boat upon the sea, while the fishermen were hastily putting out another to overtake us.

Poor Sarah! "To her dying day," as she said when she told the tale, she never could forget the terror of recognising her two naughty little charges in the small figures which were seated in the far-off boat.

Very soon, however, the men had us back

and safely landed, feeling very much ashamed and not a little frightened.

After that it was a whole long week before we were allowed to go down to the sea, which seemed very hard, though we knew we deserved the sentence. Oh, how tired we got of walking in the town or along the parade with our best dresses on, and Sarah prim and stiff between us, instead of scampering on the shingle and paddling in the water and poking about in the sea-weed for crabs and shrimps, though we never caught any.

By the time we were trusted again, our holiday was nearly gone; but we talked it all over in long winter nights. And when years had passed away, and Willie and I were both grown tall and grave and full of other thoughts and cares, we often laughed at the remembrance of the pleasures and also of the scrapes we had together.

The Captain's Monkey.

ONCE or twice in every year I had to pay a visit to a cousin of my father's, who was very fond of children in general, and of me, her god-daughter, in particular.

I was not very much delighted when the invitation came; but as I only had to stay three or four days, and Cousin Eleanor spoilt me exceedingly, I submitted to be prepared, and started in good spirits for the little town which was but a short drive from home.

To me then it seemed quite a busy place, but I believe now that it was a sleepy town enough, and even the tradesmen were of the "take it easy" species.

Cousin Eleanor's was as neat and trim a house as ever a maiden lady inhabited, and she bore with my youthful untidinesses with a patience that must have been heroic; more than I can say of old Hannah, her confidential servant.

There was a certain formula to be gone through upon the occasion of each visit, so that I knew exactly all that would happen from the time the carriage set me down at the door until the moment when I bade farewell to Cousin Eleanor.

First of all I was kissed and welcomed, and Hannah was called upon to remark how much I had grown, and how the resemblance to my great-aunt Alethea became more striking each month and year.

Next I was conducted upstairs to a trim little bedroom, where Hannah removed my walking-things, smoothed my hair, tied my pinafore, and finally conveyed me to the parlour, where Cousin Eleanor sat knitting—always knitting, except in the evenings, when she took up netting for a change.

I always took a doll with me when I went

to Heath Villa (I never could understand how
the little house came by its name), and arriving
in the parlour with her in my arms was the
signal for a short inquiry as to my progress in
needlework, the subject suggested by the dainty
dresses my "child" wore.

Next I sat down in the window and gazed
across the street to where "Jay and Son,
Undertakers," lived. Not a cheerful prospect
opposite one's dwelling, yet for me this under-
taker's shop had a strange fascination, for which
I cannot now account, and all manner of dreamy
fancies passed through my mind when I heard
the hammering of the men at work, which is
surely like no other hammering.

I knew they were working at some coffin,
and in imagination I would follow that coffin
to its destination; sometimes to a house where
little children were crying for a mother who
would never smile upon them more; sometimes
to a darkened room where a tiny infant form
lay still and cold in death; sometimes to a
house where there was no one to mourn—no
one to weep for him who was laid in that
straight, narrow bed I had listened to the

making of in "Jay and Son's" shop. So, you see, I was what people call a strange child, to have these thoughts and fancies, and even to feel a sort of happiness, or rather interest in them; one which not unfrequently ended in bringing tears to my eyes, which Cousin Eleanor perceiving, set herself to find me some amusement, lest I should be dull away from home.

That amusement would be a huge scrap-book, which I turned over until I heard Hannah coming to lay the cloth for dinner—always a pleasant interlude in the programme of that first day's occupation. After I had slept one night in the little white-curtained bed, I felt more at home, and the consciousness that my visit was half-made went far to raise my spirits, so that I grew actually frisky by its close, although never so far forgetting decorum as to lose my character of being "a dear, good child, and no trouble whatever."

I am not perfectly sure if Hannah agreed in that last clause, for I know I occasioned her sundry trips into the parlour with a short brush and dust-pan, to "take up" my stray crumbs, or remove the dust which my active feet had brought in from outdoors. However, in my hearing she made no uncomplimentary remark, and perhaps I was mistaken in supposing that a load was lifted from her mind when my visit was over.

But there came a time when a real diversion took place in the routine of the three days, and it was about that I meant to tell you when I began.

I had commenced my customary survey of Mr. Jay's establishment, and was straining my ears to catch the familiar "tap, tap" of the hammers when Cousin Eleanor exclaimed:

"I wonder if the captain's monkey will come to the window."

"A monkey—a captain!" I cried excitedly.

"Yes, love" (Cousin Eleanor always called me some such fond epithet, and I often wished she wouldn't). "There is a gentleman lodging opposite—the little house next to Jay's. He is a captain, so Hannah tells me, and I believe Sykes the butcher told her; at any rate he is some seafaring man, one may be sure, by the look of him, and his foreign-looking trunks and packages, to say nothing of a grey parrot and a monkey. For my part, I wonder any one would take him in as a lodger; but it is said that he is some distant relation of Mrs. Slater's come from abroad."

Here was startling intelligence indeed!

A sailor—a captain perhaps—with a parrot and a real, live monkey, to be lodging in that dull little town. Wonders would never cease!

For that once I had no thought to spare for Jay's coffins or their fancied occupants; neither did I require to be amused with the scrap-book. I sat watching for a peep at the captain's monkey until dinner was on the table, and resumed my post the moment I had put back my chair into its usual place after the meal was concluded, according to the habit Hannah had inculcated.

Just before tea-time I " saw the captain "—a bronzed, weather-beaten man, who could be none other than a sailor; but the monkey remained invisible to my anxious eyes.

If it had not been for hope of what the morrow might bring forth, I believe I should have cried when the shutters were closed that evening; the game at backgammon seemed weary work, and I was not at all sorry when Hannah appeared, to say it was bedtime.

After breakfast I had to run six times round the garden at the back of the house—Cousin Eleanor said it was good exercise—then I had to hem a duster, as a proof that needlework was not neglected in my home education; next I had to go for a walk, which terminated in a call upon an old lady who always wished me to be taken to see her when I came to Heath Villa, because she had known my mother when *she* was a little girl. At last these duties were accomplished, and, doll in arms, I sat down to watch for the monkey.

A quarter of an hour passed, twenty minutes, twenty-five—no monkey. The captain had gone out, Mrs. Slater was peacefully reading in the bow-window with her spectacles on, and I began to wonder which room contained the interesting visitor, for Hannah told me that some of the townspeople had seen it hanging out at a front window on more than one occasion.

My eyes must have wandered as well as my thoughts, for I never noticed when it was that a little knot of people began to collect before our opposite neighbour's house, with their gaze directed upwards, as if perhaps the chimney might have been on fire.

Probably Mrs. Slater had some such fear, for I saw her remove her spectacles, lay down her book and, after a surprised glance at the people in the street, cross the room evidently for the purpose of ringing up Bridget.

I suppose the inquiry produced some soothing reassurance, for the spectacles were resumed and the book reopened, though ever and again Mrs. Slater glanced towards the window, doubtless surprised at the breach of politeness which her fellow-townspeople were guilty of in planting themselves before her house.

I looked, Cousin Eleanor looked, Hannah looked, but we did not look high enough; not so high as a window in the roof, at which the monkey was disporting itself in a change of costumes belonging to Mrs. Slater's servant.

It was only when a crowd had gathered —a crowd, that is to say, for a small country town, not a London crowd—that we became

aware of the performance which was drawing
shouts of laughter from the bystanders.

Out ran Mrs. Slater at last, out ran Bridget.
Horror of horrors! the monkey's face grinned
from within the frills of her night-cap: her
shawl, her bonnet, her afternoon gown, were
all in turn adjusted and then torn off. The
wretched animal brushed its head with her
brush, stood glass "in hand" and surveyed
the result, cleaned its teeth and rinsed its
mouth, and performed antics which made even
staid old Hannah laugh till the tears came
into her eyes. And the worst of it was that
no one could do anything to stay the work of
destruction, no one felt disposed to enter the
dwelling and capture the mischievous creature,
who had in some way escaped from the apartment allotted to him and invaded Bridget's
premises.

I am afraid I must own to excessive regret
when the captain's return put an end to the
monkey's amusements. I did not catch
another glimpse of "Jack" while my visit
lasted, and I heard that it was removed at the
close of a week to the Zoological Gardens as a

place of safe custody. All I can say is that I regretted its absence when the time came for my next visit to the quiet uneventful little town.

"Eighty-Eight."

JUST think of coming to your eighty-eighth birthday! I used to wonder how it would feel, whether I should be pleased to get presents, and above all whether any one would be able conscientiously to wish me "many happy returns of the day."

I do not suppose the idea would ever have entered my mind only that old Mrs. Yates, who lived in a tiny white cottage near our home, had reached this age, and therefore possessed an interest for me.

Such a cottage! so small, so dark, so low! Yet nothing would have persuaded the old body to move, for there she had been born and there she meant to die. She had a daughter of sixty-one, and a granddaughter of forty. These three lived together, "with never a man belonging to them," as Mrs. Yates said, for all three were widows, and well content it seemed to be so. The granddaughter took in sewing, and thus I became a visitor at the cottage, for I always begged to be taken when any work was being arranged about.

At such times, growing weary of listening to directions about "two inches longer," or "three broad and three narrow tucks," I would wander out into the garden and pay a visit to Mrs. Yates, who on sunny days sat under the shade of one of the tall trees in an arm-chair which was even older I believe than herself.

She used to call me to her, and take my hand in her wrinkled old hand and say, "Pretty dear," and shake her head. I wonder if any dim memory could have been floating in her mind of days when she too was a child?

Her daughter took a pride in relating the incidents of the old lady's life, of how she had been in foreign parts ("furrin," Eliza called them) but had found no place like the cottage, "no place like home." So there she dwelt with her father and mother, working at her needle and ironing and clear-starching for the squire's family; and then when young William Yates married her, he joined the group round the cottage fire, so that her parents never lost their daughter. Afterwards little children came, but all except Eliza died young, and in course of time the old people were carried out of the narrow doorway and laid in the churchyard. Of her father Eliza said little, so I made my own guesses as to the time and manner of his death, which were I dare say highly improbable; any details about Eliza personally, or her daughter Jane Eliza, possessed no charm in my ears—all interest was centred in the old woman of eighty-eight.

But a sad termination came to the story of the aged life and the ancient cottage. One night there was a fire to be seen from our back windows, and it proved to be Mrs. Yates' dwelling which was blazing away under the quiet summer sky. No one ever found out how the accident originated which levelled the poor little place and broke the old woman's heart.

She was not hurt, neither had she appeared so very much frightened when they roused her up and carried her through the clouds of smoke out of the little door into the garden, and thence to the nearest neighbour's.

But uninjured in body, poor Mrs. Yates could not recover the shock of hearing that she had lost her much-loved cottage. A subscription was raised for her, which quickly reached a sum sufficient to put them in a far more comfortable dwelling, but the old woman sank into a helpless imbecility and died in a fortnight's time. With tears in her eyes, Eliza brought me an old, old teapot, one of the few things saved from the general destruction, which she said was her mother's greatest treasure, and had "been in the family" more than a hundred years. I have it yet, this old cracked teapot; with its painted ladies in yellow gowns, green shawls, and red bonnets, and gentlemen in blue and brown. Not transparent, beautiful, almost priceless dragon-china, handed down from royalty perhaps to one after another of a noble family, but still I prize it in memory of the old woman of eighty-eight who sat on sunny days in the shady cottage garden when I was a little child.

The cottage was never rebuilt, the trees were pulled down long ago, and I believe three or four modern villas have risen into being upon the piece of land where once was nothing more valuable than cabbages, French beans, and rhubarb.

I *believe* so, for I have never seen it. I would rather keep the old place in my thoughts as it used to be, and fancy paints it in the bright tints of a time that can never be renewed.

A Sprained Ankle.

HAVE you ever sprained yours? Do you know how bad it is, and how the only consolation is to have it happen in lesson-time, because it insures you a week's holiday at the very least—perhaps three!

I have met with this disaster, and I am going to tell you how it came about.

There was some talk of our leaving our home; it ended in talk, I am glad to say; yet for a week or two it seemed as if we really were very likely to remove to The Chase, which was ten miles away.

One day lessons seemed very unusually troublesome. I was plodding through the

French verb "Aimer," and speculating as to the use of committing it to memory, when the door opened and my mother's face seemed to herald a half holiday even before she spoke of it.

It was spring — late spring, when the weather has been all it ought to be, and you know *that* means something almost better than summer. Just the day to see The Chase, and there we must drive as early in the afternoon as possible, so that we might be home before night set in.

How sweet and fresh the air was, and how I enjoyed the rapid pace of the over-fed under-worked ponies as they dashed along, not even slackening speed much when we came to the steep hill leading into the village of Woodbridge, which was within sight of The Chase.

All round were the green fields and slopes; the house itself was a charming place, looking out from a nest of trees upon a velvet lawn, shining evergreens, and beds gay with bright spring flowers.

The furniture of the late owner had not

been removed, and as I followed my mother from room to room, I began wondering whose feet had trodden on those soft carpets and fleecy rugs; whether they had been young feet whose owners did not like to go away from their beautiful home when death came in to change it all.

Rapidly we passed through the house, which was evidently too large for us, just glancing at the portraits in the hall, and the choice pictures in some of the rooms, lingering longest of all in the garden where there were such lovely clumps of azalea and rhododendron. By the time we were in the carriage the sun was beginning to sink low, much to mamma's anxiety; but the ponies were in high spirits after their rest and feed, starting at a pace which promised us an arrival at home before it was really dark.

I had no great anxiety about Turk and Tom's vagaries, for I was used to them; I was conscious of the pleasurable sensation of passing swiftly through the air, which was so soft and fragrant, and it set me dreaming as usual. In a vague indefinite way I felt as if God and heaven were nearer to us in the quiet evening twilight than in the glare and gleam of day, and all sorts of longings and purposes sprang up within me to be good, to be less unworthy of the blessings and joys which filled my life. I began reviewing my days. Neglected duties started up to reproach me, even careless practising, smeared copies, bad exercises, "cobbled" sewing, were like gaunt, grim, unwelcome phantoms, and I resolved to have no more of them in the future—I would "turn over a new leaf."

A jerk, a quick swaying of the little carriage, and I was in the ditch by the road-side —happily for me and Clotilda, my favourite doll, a dry one!

I was too much astonished to cry; I did not even know I was hurt until they moved me, and then—well, I knew no more until I found myself on the sofa at home with mamma and two or three servants round me, and a smell of eau-de-Cologne and wine and water everywhere. I found out then that I had fallen with my foot doubled under me, and the result was a sprained ankle.

The doctor came, and there was a great deal of bandaging; and when he said it "was not very bad," I thought how little he knew about it, and what a disagreeable, unfeeling creature he was. Not very bad indeed! with that shooting pain coming every time I tried to move, and very often when I kept still too.

For a whole week I must lie on a sofa in the dressing-room, and be patient—so they told me. I wonder if people know how hard it is when you want to go out, or to play, or to do everything you *can't* do, just to be told, "Be patient."

However, there was no help for it; I was forced to lie still, and not for a week only but for a fortnight. It is only fair to own, though, that I might have been well sooner but for my own fault. One evening I felt better; the pain was gone, and I was so sure I could walk if only I was allowed to try, that when the opportunity came I *did* try, and the attempt ended in a disaster.

Mamma had been reading to me; the book was "Cloister Legends," and I always think of those legends when I hear of a sprained ankle;

but she was called away, and as I heard her going downstairs it seemed an excellent moment for the trial of my walking powers.

Very cautiously I slipped myself along to the end of the sofa; cautiously, too, I put one hand on the table and rose to a standing position. Certainly a twinge of pain, but not much; I took one step, only one, and my poor injured foot gave way beneath me, and with a sharp cry I fell back, and did not even know who came in and laid me down again, so faint was I.

You may be sure I had a longer lecture than ever about patience, and I felt very much ashamed of myself, *so* ashamed that I did not grumble any more about lying still.

However, all things come to an end, even disagreeable ones such as sprained ankles, and it was not so very long before I was running about the same as ever, all the pain and the weariness forgotten. By that time it was quite settled that we should not remove from our dear old home, far dearer to me than The Chase, though not half so large or half so grand.

And about the good resolutions which were in progress of formation during that drive home? Well, I am afraid that I forget them sadly often; it is so easy to make plans for improvement, and so difficult to carry them out! Happy is it for us that One Who is very good, and kind, and patient, looks down well pleased even upon a child's little efforts to do better— those small and often weak efforts which will, however, if persevered in, gain us in the end a victory over self.

I forgot to say that Clotilda, who shared my fall, only damaged her nose very slightly, so that I was compelled to " pretend " a sprained ankle for her. She preserved a smiling face through all her suffering, never spoke an impatient word, nor—like her little mother—delayed her recovery by a wilful and rash action in a word, she was a " model doll."

Dr. Syntax.

THAT was the name I gave our doctor —*why* I cannot tell you, because he was not at all like the pictures in the old books of Dr. Syntax—yet so I called him, and so in my thoughts I call him now.

His hair was as white as snow, but his face was rather young. I have heard that he grew white in a few hours, very, very sad hours they were; but I cannot be quite sure if this is true, because it happened before I was born.

My Dr. Syntax was very kind to children—he did not send them a great deal of medicine, and I really believe he felt sorry for them and tried to make it as nice as he could; perhaps he did not like taking it himself. When I went to tea with the little Williamsons who lived near us, I used to wish I might taste *their* medicine. No ugly pills, but dear pretty, tiny white sweets, like "hundreds and thousands"—why no one could cry, or want something to take the taste out, if the dose had been a whole bottleful, instead of three of these delightful "gobules."

The Williamsons' nurse called them "go-balls." I don't remember once when I was there, but some of the children had to take something out of this pretty medicine-chest. One was feverish, one had a headache, one could not eat her dinner, or one was going to have a cold, or it was earache, or tooth-ache—always something to bring Mrs. Williamson into the nursery with the "go-balls."

The children would stand round eyeing the tiny bottles wistfully, and little Carrie always cried: "Me some, me some," and put out the tip of her tongue to receive what she longed for.

Well, that was not the kind of medicine I had to take—Dr. Syntax did not believe in it, and so we did not believe in it either, only I wished in that respect that I had been born a Williamson.

Though I was very fond of our Dr. Syntax, there were times when I was angry with him, and those times were when mamma or any one was ill, and he insisted upon the house being kept quiet.

"Not a sound which can be avoided, *perfect* rest, *perfect* quiet, and we shall do very well." Many a time I have heard him give these directions (looking meaningly at me if I was visible), and then run downstairs with the very creakingest of boots, banging the door behind him before any one could get into the hall.

But now I must tell you the reason every one liked Dr. Syntax. Not only because he was clever, and had a "large practice," but because he was so kind and unselfish—kindest, above all, to the very poor.

There were not so many of this class round that part; but such as there were to be called poor, were very, very low and miserable.

One of these, a young girl, was ill. She was a stranger, "a regular tramp," the servants said, who had come to the neighbourhood no one knew why, and taken a miserable cellar-like kitchen in one of the worst parts, by the river-side.

I suppose she was ill when she came; perhaps it was some feeling of illness which made her stop on her journey, and take the damp kitchen in "Elizabeth Row." However, two days after, every one round knew that the strange girl was seized with fever.

This news did not travel as far as our house, and the other gentlemen's houses, for about a week; I am telling you now what we afterwards heard, when rich and poor were grieving for "Dr. Syntax."

I have always thought that the very lowest and poorest people were kind to each other in trouble; indeed, I am sure of it. But in this case every one was afraid to go near the sick girl—even the parish doctor, so it was said.

In some way the news of this terrible fever reached Dr. Syntax, and leaving his richer patients to the care of his partner for a few hours, he went to see the sick girl.

"You'd best not go in, sir," said the woman of the house. "It's terrible catching-like, and nothing can save her—you've no call to risk your own life."

Dr. Syntax was not often angry, but he looked very angry then, I suppose, as he motioned the woman aside and went into the fever-tainted atmosphere of this miserable kitchen.

She was quite young, this poor friendless creature who lay there on a heap of rags for her only bed—very young to be dying there in such lonely misery.

Dr. Syntax saw that all hope was gone, and yet he could not bear to turn away and leave her so. He was so good that he thought more of what would come after death than anything else, and he wanted to wait lest she grew conscious at the last, so that he might say to her some little word of One Who had died to save souls, and might try to win from her one prayer for pardon for the sins of her life.

So our doctor stayed on in the cellar-kitchen, as the day faded and deepened into night. He knew that all those who needed him elsewhere would be cared for, and it seemed to me just like what is said in the Scriptures about he who "leaves the ninety-nine sheep, to seek the one which was lost."

It was as he expected—just before the end came she ceased her rambling talk, and knew that some friendly face was near her; listened, too, to the few words he had to speak.

And then she died, this poor unknown girl; and many people said that the doctor's brave devotion had been in vain; but I cannot believe *that*. Who can measure God's mercy, or man's repentance—even the repentance of the last moment? and besides, our doctor had done what he could, and nothing so done for God can ever be in vain.

So Dr. Syntax went back to his home, with his thoughts running upon the girl he had seen die. Home, but he could not sleep, nor eat—in fact he knew that the fever was coming upon him.

I don't suppose he regretted what he had done; he had long before lost his wife and child, and had no near relation to grieve for him. While he felt the power to do it, he set all his affairs in order, and then lay down to die.

I could not tell you the excitement which spread around and about for many a mile, as soon as it was known that the good doctor's life was in danger. His house was surrounded by the poor, waiting, watching for good news —the good news which never came.

But when it was told that the brave warm heart had ceased to beat, that the clear bright eye was closed in death, women and children, and even strong men wept for sorrow that there was one friend the less for them in this busy world which does not hold too many firm, true friends for any of us.

I shall never forget the crowd which followed him to the grave. Such a sight had never been seen, they said, in our part of the world; and I, peeping from behind the drawn blinds of an upper window, sobbed out in the bitterness of my childish grief:

"Oh, mamma, there can never, never be another Dr. Syntax."

MY GOLDEN DAYS.

BY

M. F. S.,

AUTHOR OF "CATHERINE HAMILTON," "THE THREE WISHES,"
"STORIES OF THE SAINTS," "CATHERINE GROWN OLDER,"
"FLUFFY," "LEGENDS OF THE SAINTS," "STORIES
OF MARTYR PRIESTS," "TOM'S CRUCIFIX,"
ETC., ETC.

✳✳✳

London:
R. WASHBOURNE, 18 PATERNOSTER ROW.
1878.

Contents.

Third Series.

	PAGE
WET DAYS	5
"ROUSSEAU'S DREAM"	13
"NERVES"	21
OUR FIRSTS OF MAY	33
TOM, DICK, AND HARRY	42
GREAT-UNCLE HUGH	49
LONG DRESSES	58

MY GOLDEN DAYS.

Wet Days.

I DO not like them now, and I am sure I liked them even less when I was a child. We know that the rain is wanting for the flowers, and fruit, and crops; but I never found it any comfort to be told "how glad the farmer was" of the wet day, when *I* was feeling so very sorry.

Neither did it help me to be advised to "employ myself." It was just what I wished to do, only I could not find the way, and no one gave me an idea. Of course there was always sewing to be had for the asking, but as this was never a pleasant task, I did not like it for the occupation of a wet day, when it seems the time, of all others, you want something pleasant to do.

My governess made me write out a piece of poetry about wet days once, as a cure for complaining of them. I don't remember all of it, but it ran thus:

> "*She* loves a rainy day who sweeps the hearth,
> And threads the busy needle, or applies
> The scissors to the torn or threadbare sleeve;
> Who blesses God that she has friends and home;
> Who, in the pelting of the storms, will think
> Of some poor neighbour that she can befriend.
> Who trims the lamp at night, and reads aloud
> To a young brother tales he loves to hear,
> Such are not sad, even on a rainy day."

I was ten years, and perhaps a little more, when I scrawled that in a round hand, ornamented with a few smears, splutters, and blots in my copybook, and when done it gave me neither comfort nor example, as Miss Morgan expected.

"Sweeps the hearth." Well, that was expressly forbidden ever since I once set the broom on fire.

"Threads the busy needle." I have already explained that this was misery of the most intense kind to me, nor had I any young brother who required tales read to him.

Clearly, then, I must invent an amusement for myself, as it was impossible to get a suggestion.

I have before now told you of the pleasures of play-cookery, for my dolls—"messing," as the servants called it. But upon a dreary day, with the rain pouring down incessantly, Clotilda, Angeline, and the rest of my family were left to repose in their several beds and drawers, so that cooking for them was unnecessary.

It came into my mind, one drenching November day, how delightful it would be to do "real" pastry and cake-making, to manufacture puddings which could be eaten without an effort; to see marvellous jellies and blancmanges come to table, and listen with the delighted feeling of well-earned success, to the praise bestowed by those who partook of the dainties.

"Mamma, may I ask cook to teach me to make things?"

No wonder a look of bewilderment spread over my mother's face at this sudden demand breaking in upon the letters she was writing for the out-going New York mail.

"*Things*, mamma!—real pies, and cakes, and things. I'm tired of everything, and I want to learn cooking."

"But I don't feel sure that cook will agree," said mamma, when she grasped my meaning.

"Oh, I'll coax her;" and I was gone, to be recalled before I had closed the door.

"And your lessons ?"

"All done, mamma. I may go into the kitchen, may I ?"

So I gained my point, and descended to do my utmost in persuading cook into a good temper.

"Cooky dear, I want something to do, it's so dull."

"This isn't the place for young ladies, miss. What would you think if *I* was to come walking into your schoolroom ?"

"I should be very glad to see you, cook; it would be a change," said I, hoping she would take the hint and express herself pleased at my appearance. But she didn't — only bustled about from cupboard to dresser, and dresser to fire, while I stood on one leg eying her wistfully.

"Come, missy, go upstairs like a good child. Here are some raisins and currants for your messes, if that's what you've come for, and a lump of sugar."

I should have been grateful enough only a day or two before, though she did say "messes;" but now I shook my head, and did not attempt to take the offered raisins.

"I don't want them. I want to stay here and see you. I know you've got a cake to make, and pastry, and ever so many things, and I want to learn, and mamma says yes; and, oh, cook dear, dear cook, please let me."

It came out hurriedly, breathlessly, and then I waited the result with beating heart.

"Your mamma says yes, miss? Well-a-day, what next? Young ladies should be sitting at the pianner, or doing their worsted-work, if they knew their place; however, if the missis says so you may stay—*for once* though, mind, miss."

"Yes, I'll mind. Oh, you dear old thing," I

cried, seizing her round the neck, and striving to dance her up and down the kitchen, though with difficulty, for I was small and cook was stout.

"Now, miss, leave off that nonsense, or upstairs you'll go," she cried, as she settled her cap which I had somewhat disarranged. "Stand still while I tie an apron round you, or a fine mess you'll be in."

I sobered down under the threat of being ejected from the kitchen, and submitted to be tied up in a huge white apron, which came out of the dresser-drawer. With many warnings not to touch a thing, cook began her pastry-making, and I watched her intently and so quietly that with unusual good temper she gave me a little lump of paste, produced a small pie-dish, and directed me how to roll out my crust and cover my fruit, so that one of the apple-tarts should be my own making. After the crowning joy of marking the edge all round with a fork, it was put in the oven, and I went upstairs happier, and wiser too, than I had entered the kitchen.

Surely I was never more pleased or proud

than when my little apple-pie appeared at dinner-time. I looked with affection upon each print of the fork. I believe I would not have had it cut for the world, excepting that my admiration was tempered with anxiety as to its flavour. I pressed mamma to be candid with me—was it really nice, or did she "only say so?" was there too much sugar, or perhaps too little? did she really like the flavour of cloves, or would she have preferred lemon-peel? With such and the like questions I plied her, and she eat a piece of my little apple-tart, pronouncing it delicious.

Well, that was the beginning of cooking on wet days. It grew into an institution in spite of cook's prejudices, and from that time until I was a young lady with plaited hair and tails to my dresses, I used to look forward to a wet day spent in the kitchen. Oh, what fun I have had making out receipts from cook's own manuscript-book, a perfect marvel of bad spelling and writing, and how pleased she grew with my success, delighting in the lightness of "missie's pastry," and the excellence of "missie's cakes," as much and even more than missie herself.

"No rose without a thorn," says the proverb, and the trying part of my practice in cookery was the pretended horror and disgust with which my father and Charlie would taste some extra-special culinary experiment about which my anxiety was intense.

I think I see them now, pulling wry faces, coughing, asking for water with an appearance of suffering which for the moment deceived me; still this was a very brief and passing drawback to my pleasure, and I advise you little folks to get mamma's consent, and then persuade *your* "cooky" to tie you up in an apron, and let you into kitchen mysteries as a fine amusement, and a useful one too, for some of *your* wet days.

"Rousseau's Dream."

I HAD outgrown the instruction-book and been promoted to easy pieces, and I was supposed to be "getting on nicely," at the time that I was given "Rousseau's Dream," with variations, to practise.

I did not think it a pretty air—not half so pretty as many others already learned, neither did I see the duty of perfecting myself in it just to please grandmamma, who had played it herself in her own young days. So I am afraid I was very graceless and unwilling in setting about my task, and my aversion to the piece grew so strong that I almost hated the time spent at the piano.

Grandmamma did not live with us, but in one of the southern counties of England, where we visited her each summer. "Goodmayes" was the name of the house, a pretty, old-fashioned place, with high laurel hedges on either side of the garden walks, great bushes of red, white, blush and damask roses, sweet-williams, larkspurs, honeysuckle, white lilies, tiger-lilies, and all the sweet flowers which grow in "grandmothers' gardens," but not often in ours of the present day.

Everything about and around grandmamma was antique, or she would not have liked it. Perhaps this was why, when I had played my little selection of modern "airs," she declared that nothing came up in tunefulness to the melodies of her girlish days, and it was then she asked me to learn "Rousseau's Dream."

"To please me," she said, and I ought to have done it willingly—as willingly as she gratified all my wishes when I stayed at Goodmayes.

The twelve months slipped by; it was time for us to pay our usual visit, and the much-disliked piece of music was very imperfectly known.

Mamma looked grave when, at her request, I played it over the day before we started.

"You could certainly do better than *that*," she said. "I am afraid the will is wanting. Grandmamma will think you do not care to please her."

"It is such an ugly, stupid, tiresome tune," I said, half-angry, half-crying. "It goes dinging, dinging on. I hate the sound of it."

"I should have thought you would take pleasure in pleasing others," was my mother's reply.

"I can practise it up at Goodmayes," I remarked feeling somewhat ashamed.

"Yes, but you have had a whole year to get ready this little pleasure for grandmamma, and it will not be at all the same thing if she hears you learning it after you arrive. I dare say *she* has been thinking of everything which could give you happiness. Grandmamma is so unselfish."

This was a home-thrust. *I* had been selfish, and I knew it, and was vexed and uncomfortable accordingly, and yet I still felt injured at the mention of "Rousseau's Dream." Why had that tune, above all others, been chosen as grandmamma's favourite?

There was a cloud over my spirits such as I had never been oppressed by in previous years when we were starting for Goodmayes; even the warm June sunshine seemed to have lost its brightness for me, and the pretty scenery through which the train whirled us, looked flat and unattractive, and all because the neglect of "Rousseau's Dream" weighed upon my conscience!

See what comes of not doing one's duty even in a matter which may appear very small. It is the faithfulness in "little things" that gives peace and content to us all.

Has it ever seemed to you that the very outside of a house has something strange about it when there is trouble within? Perhaps it was one of my childish fancies, and yet as we drove up to the gates of Goodmayes, I had a sort of consciousness that something was amiss.

This consciousness became a certainty when Pearson, the old gardener, hurried forward with the shadow of some coming trouble on his wrinkled face.

"If you'd not mind walking up to the house," he said confusedly; "the missis is taken bad, and every noise disturbs her; she'd be sure to hear the wheels."

Yes, poor grandmamma had been indeed "taken bad" in the night, and she would never in this world be any better.

All day—so the servants told us—she had been talking of our coming and seeing that everything was made ready; "and she was looking to hear missie play to her so nicely," said Haines, thereby unconsciously giving me a terrible twinge of remorse.

At night poor old grandmamma had gone to rest in her usual health, but an hour later she was seized with a sudden pain in her head, and a stroke of paralysis had followed. We could not see her then; later my mother went quietly in and sat there unrecognised for some hours.

Towards the last, memory awakened, and we saw by her glance she knew us all; but she could not speak to us, and on the second day after we reached Goodmayes poor grandmamma died.

I never played "Rousseau's Dream" again.

✱✱✱

I could not bear to think of it. But my mother made me keep it always to remind me of my selfish disregard of poor grandmamma's wish; and to this day, when I turn over an old music-book in which the piece is bound up, its yellow pages seem to tell me of the sorrow and regret which may follow on a little duty unfulfilled.

It seemed as if no one cared to live at Goodmayes long when it passed into other hands. Tenant after tenant left it, and when I saw the old white house some years ago, it was in a dilapidated condition indeed. The monthly roses which grew outside grandmamma's breakfast-room window were there still and in luxuriant bloom, but a row of rough heads appeared above them, and we found that the house was tenanted by some five or six families of the poor of that part, who lived there almost rent free.

Clothes hung drying upon lines stretched across the paths, which once old Pearson weeded so carefully; nothing seemed left excepting the straggling untrimmed rose-bushes, and huge clumps of lavender.

So I turned away from Goodmayes with tears in my eyes and an aching heart, and going back to my home I opened my music-book at "Rousseau's Dream," and thought of grandmamma, and tried to let the lesson sink deep down into my 'mind, which the remembrance of her must always bring.

"Nerves."

I USED to think that the most terrible calamity which could befall a living creature must be to have "*nerves*." I have heard that an old woman once said she "thanked God she was born before nerves were invented;" and I believe I shared her feelings of gratitude when I was a child, or rather I *should* have done, if I had known about it.

The cause of my extreme horror and alarm at the thought of nerves was certainly Miss White, an old, old friend of my mother's, who used to visit us sometimes. While I was very small I had an indistinct idea that Miss White was a person who had been—or who was—very unhappy, because if ever Charlie and I laughed at her funny dress or grumbled at the length of her visit, nurse used to say we were very naughty children, and bid us "be sorry for the poor lady."

The first day she came was not so bad, for we felt a little shy, and were therefore unusually quiet, but when the strangeness wore off, (which was generally on the second morning, or *certainly* upon the third,) we were apt to try Miss White's nerves by our method of amusing ourselves.

Don't you think it was hard when one woke up very fresh after a long night, that all singing or running about, or even jumping out of bed to fetch something you wanted to read, were forbidden, because Miss White slept in the room underneath, and her "nerves" would not bear the least confusion or noise before breakfast? So it was through the day. As surely as we were having a romp in the nursery, so surely did a message arrive begging that like "dear good children" we would play at some quiet game because of "poor Miss White."

In our ordinary way of life I was a great deal in my mother's company—after I had outgrown a nurse I mean. When Miss White was paying one of her long visits, these same nerves of hers were apt to be distressed if I were in the room, no matter how quietly employed, and after a while she was sure to say, "Don't you think, my dear, that little folks are best upstairs?"

I almost hated her when she said that, neither could I bear to hear her call mamma "my dear;" in fact every word she spoke gave me a cross, out-of-temper-ish feeling, which I dare say you all know as well as I do.

This dislike to Miss White had grown so strong that mamma said at last she would tell me something about her life, which would make me pity her, and bear her tiresome ways without complaining.

I remember how anxiously I waited for this coming story, until one twilight evening in winter, mamma said she would not try my patience any longer—I certainly should hear about Miss White's early days. I poked the fire into a blaze, and arranged myself cosily on the rug. I *did* love twilight stories, especially when my curiosity was roused; and this is much about the way mamma began :

"When I knew Miss White first, she was a very pretty girl of about fourteen, and full of merriment and fun."

"Dear me, how she must have changed!" said I.

"I was younger," my mother went on, without heeding the interruption, "a great deal younger, yet I was at school and she was my 'school mamma.'"

"I shouldn't like her for mine," was my next remark.

"How good she was to me I could never tell you, and of course I looked up to her as the most clever of all the great girls at Miss Mortimer's establishment for young ladies—the prettiest and the merriest every one knew she was!

"I suppose school-days are always pleasant to look back upon—we forget the troubles and see a golden radiance shining over the time which has gone for ever; and perhaps that is why I think that few schools of the present day are like Miss Mortimer's.

"We had to study hard, but the principle there was,

> "'Work while you work,
> Play while you play;'

and accordingly we *did* enjoy ourselves in recreation times.

"Once or twice in the summer, either just before or just after the holidays, we used to have a picnic to Carlton Wood, which was only a drive from the town.

"Miss Mortimer engaged a private omnibus and two or three carriages from the Red Lion, and the whole party of girls and teachers went off for a long day in the wood.

"You can imagine the excitement for a day or two beforehand, the hopes and fears about the weather, the eager examination of the barometer in the hall, the questioning of Miss Mortimer, mademoiselle, the English teacher, the gardener—*every one* in fact, in and around the house, as to whether they *thought* it would rain.

"Once or twice we roused up to see a drenching morning; but for the most part, I believe, the weather was very kind to us on picnic days.

"The big girls took charge of the little ones,—every 'mamma' of her own child in particular—and thus it fell to Nellie White's lot to keep guard over me.

"Upon the day I am going to tell you of, a tiresome freak was upon me, and I declared that I *would not* sit by Nellie in the omnibus, neither would I keep within her sight when we roamed about in the wood. A new girl had come to school—*so new* that she had not been presented with a school 'child,' because that was a proof of confidence earned only by some time of probation.

"Yet Katie James was old enough to rank among the mothers; and when I declared that I should stay with her, and she said she wanted to have me, Nellie White consented to give me into her charge for an hour or two, but only on condition of her being very careful.

"I did not feel very happy as I danced along by Katie's side into the shadows of the old wood—a grieved look in Nellie's eyes haunted me; still I was gratified at the notice this new girl bestowed upon me, and I tried to convince myself that I was not ungrateful to my 'school mamma.'

"For a time Katie talked and chatted with me; but she had not Nellie's untiring, unselfish patience, and, growing weary of my continuous stream of questions and remarks, she sat down on the felled trunk of an old tree and, bidding me amuse myself, began reading a book she drew from her pocket.

"It was very nice for a few minutes to do as I pleased, but I grew dull. It was all very well to say I 'could amuse myself,' but I did not know how, when all the other girls had dispersed in different directions, and Katie kept her eyes upon her book in utter disregard of anything I might say or do.

"Presently I saw that a little stream ran just below—a narrow little stream, yet much deeper than I thought as I stole quietly down to its brink.

"I began picking flowers and throwing them upon the running, rippling water, wondering where they would float to and how soon they would be carried as far as Elthover, where I knew the stream grew into a river. I had a little basket with me, and by a sudden and unfortunate inspiration I decided to send this upon the same journey laden with flowers, which perhaps some child at Elthover would get, and wonder how far they had travelled and who had sent them.

"No sooner thought of than done! hastily cramming in handfuls of wild flowers, I launched my basket upon the stream and stood watching it with delighted eyes. Only for a moment though, and the delight [changed to regret, and my longing after my possession was such that I resolved to recover it if possible.

"It did not seem as if it could be difficult or dangerous to go down to the edge, 'make a long arm,' and seize the basket—at any rate I would try.

"One glance at Katie, who sat dreamily over her story-book—no, she did not see me, nor would she be any the wiser when I had accomplished my purpose in safety. I went down to the brink cautiously enough; the basket had only gone a yard or so, and seemed lingering on purpose for me to regain it if I wished. I stretched out my arm and then— well, I suppose the soft muddy bank gave way, and, loosing my footing, I fell with a shriek into the dark, deep little stream. I say *I suppose,* for I only know what they told me afterwards; and told me too how Katie roused up at my shriek and echoed it without having the sense to come to my help. Happily my faithful 'school mamma' was not far off, and, recognising the voice of her rebellious child, she darted in the direction of the stream.

"The girls have often described to me how she looked as she ran down to the edge, never speaking a word, but following where Katie pointed, her face white, her hair streaming behind her, yet silent and even calm. She never thought of fear—this brave Nellie. Plunging into the stream she held me up by the skirt of my frock until the haymakers from a field near by were brought to get us both out.

"We were carried off to the little country inn on the borders of the wood and put into bed, and by evening I was quite able to be dressed in the clothes which had been sent for, and taken back to school. Not so poor Nellie; the fright and the shock had been too much for her, and for weeks she lay at the little inn unable to be removed, with her mother and Miss Mortimer nursing her.

"It was a long time before she got well, and then she was never strong enough for school; in fact it seemed as if my wilfulness was the cause of that weak health which has been hers all her lifetime. Now, do you wonder that I love and respect Miss White, even though she has grown old and perhaps a little fidgety?"

"No, mamma, indeed. I feel as if I should almost love her myself for being so good to you; but was that really the beginning of her nerves?"

My mother laughed. I think she could not help it.

"It was the beginning of a great many troubles, my little girl. Loss of health came first, and loss of money, and friends, and home followed in after years. Miss White has had trouble enough to try *any one's* 'nerves,' and we must be very forbearing and unselfish when she visits us."

I made up my mind that I would not grumble any more, even if all my games and pleasures were stopped by Miss White's presence. I really tried to keep this resolution, too, and the mere trying helped me to find out that our visitor was far more amiable and good than I had ever thought her to be, even though she was so very unfortunate as to possess nerves!

Our Firsts of May.

PEOPLE say that the seasons are changing; when I remember our "Firsts of May" I really believe it is true. Now the month is mostly cold or very wet, even if we do not get storms of sleet every now and then; but twenty years or more ago I cannot recollect May as anything but warm and summer-like.

It was an institution in our household to give a treat to the school-children on the 1st of May, which treat was held in a field, where the small people played games and ran races, had buns and milk, and then a large slice of cake to take home with them when they had sung "God Save the Queen."

My parents took great interest in the schools. As soon as I can remember anything, it seems to me that I was taken down to see the rows of children, sometimes sewing, sometimes ciphering, or singing, which last was a great pleasure to me to listen to. It was a pleasant schoolroom, light and lofty, everything well scrubbed, and desks and forms in their places, while the walls were hung with prints and maps.

Much as I liked to visit the school-children, I don't think it ever gave me so much pleasure to stand before the rows of smiling faces and pink or lilac pinafores, as upon the day when I carried with me a little bundle of tickets which admitted their owners to the 1st of May treat.

What an excitement there was in a subdued sort of fashion! What whispering and tittering among the little people, which would soon have developed into a Babel of sound but for the warning tinkle of the school-teacher's bell, which meant " order."

Every year there was some sinner—usually a very small sinner—for whom I had to plead hard when he or she was sentenced " not to go to the treat;" and my pleading must have been effectual, for I cannot recall one instance in which any of the children were excluded.

Not only did they have games, there were prizes given for good conduct or regular attendance (I am not sure which), and for a week or two previous I had helped to arrange the smart little volumes, many of which I got leave to read beforehand.

When the time came (which time was always half-past two in the afternoon) our young visitors arrived most punctually; indeed they were more than punctual, for the field-gate was surrounded half an hour before the moment appointed for its opening.

All the girls had light frocks and smart ribbons, while the boys appeared in clean blouses, and with well-washed hands and faces. I don't believe one among them would have paid us so poor a compliment as to come dirty or untidy to our school-treat.

Though it was only a gathering of poor children, nearly all our friends who lived within an easy distance came to help amuse them; indeed, I think they enjoyed it as much as the little owners of the tickets of admission, and were quite as anxious that the 1st of May should be bright and sunny.

One year Tommy Stokes was lost going home. He was one of the infants—certainly not more than three years old—and of course his big sister should have been taking care of him. I suppose she forgot, and thought Tommy was walking along quite safely with the rest; however, when she reached her mother's gate there was no finding the little fellow, neither could any one remember exactly when and where he had last been seen.

The school-teacher stood and counted them all as they made their bows and dropped their curtsies at the gate, so Tommy had been among the children there, and Polly admitted that he was; how he slipped away or where he had wandered to, no one could guess.

The first we knew of it was when poor Miss King, the governess, arrived with an anxious, alarmed face, to ask if Tommy had been left behind. Mrs. Stokes was not long in making her appearance, looking as red as Miss King looked pale, and abusing her, Polly, and the parish in general; for she was a passionate woman, and nothing could persuade her to believe that Tommy had been fairly started on his way home.

The evenings were getting long, and as the children were dismissed early it was still perfectly light, so there was the better chance of discovering the lost child. The servants turned out to seek him; my father, mother, and of course myself went in and out among the shrubs and garden-hedges, to the field, down the lane, calling Tommy, and yet no Tommy came.

It was an unfortunate ending to our afternoon, and mamma told us afterwards that she was resolving never, never to have a school-treat again, for there was Mrs. Stokes scolding and crying in turns, Miss King white and miserable, and every one else perplexed and uneasy.

He could not be lost in broad daylight, just a little way, too, from his own home; he must be hiding surely. Yet what baby of three years old would be so naughty and mischievous as to do such a thing? He was though, little tiresome monkey!

We were giving up the search in despair, and standing by the gate looking hopelessly into each other's faces, when a merry baby laugh was heard from behind the big laurel.

"I here—Tommy here—Tommy see 'oo," it said, and there, sure enough, was the small truant, who had apparently been finding amusement in watching us run about searching for him.

When he was pulled out no one had the heart to scold him—he looked so pretty and saucy, with his large slice of cake still clutched in his tiny hand!

"For 'oo," he said, pushing the corner into his mother's mouth. "Tommy save him cake for muvver."

At this, even fiery Mrs. Stokes calmed down, and clasping her lost sheep in her arms, carried him safely home in the May twilight.

The very next year, instead of losing a child we found one—a dirty, ragged urchin, who suddenly appeared in the midst of our trim village children, no one knew how.

He was seized and questioned.

"Had he come over the fence?" No answer.

"Where did he live? where was his mother? who brought him there?"—still no answer from the small child, who eyed us without the least appearance of fear, and with his dirty hands thrust into the pockets of a pair of trousers several sizes too large for him.

We really might have believed him dumb, had not some one asked him if he should like some cake. At this he said "Yes—a jolly big piece," and began nodding his head and laughing, much more like the figure of a Chinese mandarin in my possession than anything else.

When cake and buns had been demolished, our uninvited visitor announced that his name was "Jim," and that he lived "a long way off." How and why he came, remained a mystery for ever after, though we always believed that he must have belonged to some party of tramps who wanted to be rid of the child, and so sent him in to our school-treat amongst the crowd, believing that in some way he would be cared for afterwards.

Of course we let him stay while the children played and romped and received their prizes; he was perfectly quiet and content, standing by my mother, watching all that passed with a comically "cool" look on his face, and hands still thrust into the pockets of his corduroys.

It was when "God Save the Queen" had been sung, and all the boys and girls were going home that the real difficulty came.

"Now Jim must go home too," said my mother kindly, handing him the piece of cake which was supposed to be a balm for the grief which children naturally feel when a pleasant afternoon is over.

"I've nowhere to go," said Jim stoutly, taking the cake, however, without a shadow of hesitation. "I'm to stay with you."

"But I can't keep a little boy with me," said mamma, growing puzzled. "Go away now, Jim; go home to your mother."

"Ain't got a mother. I'm going to stay with you," said Jim again; nor could he be induced to depart with the other children.

Here was a dilemma! Talk of Tommy being lost; it did not seem half such a puzzling case as Jim found!

"Come, go away, or I'll get a stick to you!"

said our old gardener, advancing towards him with a cross look upon his face.

Serenely Jim glanced upwards, and a smile shone in his dark eyes.

"Well, I'll stop with *you* then," he said; and, strange to say, Brooks took him home to his own cottage, saying he would pack him off the very next morning, "willin' or not willin'."

He didn't though! Whether he and Betsy found it was pleasant to have a little step and voice to cheer their childless home I cannot tell you; but I *can* say that Jim stayed there always, and in time became as good a gardener as old Brooks.

Neither he, nor we, ever knew who were his parents and what place was his home; all we could tell about him was what you have been told now, of the way he came amongst us as an unasked visitor upon the 1st of May.

Tom, Dick, and Harry.

ONLY a cat, a canary, and a cockatoo, and yet I consider them *quite* worthy of biographical notice in my home stories—I wonder whether you will think so too.

I have seen Manx, Angora, Persian cats of different size and colour—all handsome of course, for whose pet animal is not one of the best and handsomest of its kind? but never one which, in my opinion, surpassed our Tom, though he was of no particular family.

I don't know whether there was any striking point in his personal appearance—a finely-marked tabby of unusual size. It was his sense which gained our admiration and respect, to say nothing of his sedate, well-bred manners.

Tom had one peculiarity which was scarcely desirable—he was a born thief! Some people affirm that, if a cat is well fed it will not help itself unasked; but that is a downright delusion, for our Tom was well looked after, although meals honestly come by seemed to lack the relish which belonged to stolen goods.

And yet he went about the business in a thoughtful way; there was nothing hasty and precipitate in Tom's stealing! Even if detected, he did not hurry off with that shamefaced look you see in ordinary cats; dusters might be shaken at him, voices might rise high in tones of reproof, but Tom walked leisurely away with a reproachful glance at those who intruded upon his privacy.

Well, Tom, the cat, and Dick, the canary, were friends. Dick sometimes went by the name of the "Greenwich Pensioner," because on one sad day he got his leg smashed in a door, and hopped about on one for ever after. He was a happy little fellow for all that, and so tame that the best part of his time was spent out of the gilded cage which hung with its door open in the sunny south window of the breakfast-room.

We never could tell any one the method by which Tom and Dick were made friends. They had been young together, and whether some feeling of "auld lang syne" kept them united in maturer years I cannot say; but the surprising thing was that even as a kitten Tom never tried to make a meal of the canary. It was pretty to see the large handsome cat asleep on the rug, while the bird flitted over his head, to perch now on the fender, now on a footstool, now on the soft back of his friend.

So we come to Harry, the last of the trio of special pets—the rose-crested cockatoo which was brought home from abroad for us.

The sailor who was the bearer of the large cage said that on board ship the bird had been called Harry, so Harry he remained; but oh what trouble he gave us!

My mother wished him to have a stand—he beat about in the cage so wildly that his tail was well-nigh ruined—but when the stand came home, and Harry was chained to it, an unforeseen difficulty arose—how was he to be kept there?

Chains innumerable were tried, he bit them all through; he could unfasten a swivel in less time than it takes me to write about it, and as for the stand, it was merely something to be ruined by that sharp and all-destroying beak.

Fortunately Harry was a favourite in the kitchen, or he would certainly have retired to some bird-fancier's to reflect on his evil course. But cook took up the cudgels on his behalf when such a thing was mooted, and it gradually became an understood thing that Harry should remain loose.

After destroying all the kitchen chairs, one was reserved for his special use, and an iron bar put in place of the back, upon which he sat for hours by the fireside. Only when there was nothing of interest going on, though!

When cook was high busy, Harry was always on the edge of the table by her side, looking the picture of harmless innocence as long as she kept her eye on him, but seizing any favourable moment to assist in the operations. A second was enough for Harry to disperse a pound or two of currants about the floor: he was an adept at "topping and tailing" gooseberries, or setting his mark upon pastry. She bore with his tricks most wonderfully, did this sharp-spoken cook of ours; but then she had a warm corner in her heart for every one, even for a cockatoo.

Harry never liked me, and yet I had not consciously offended him.

When he came I was small—so small that he could not resist the temptation of pecking at my legs where they were unprotected by socks, and perhaps he felt that antipathy which birds and animals often do feel towards children.

But he did not cast aside this ill-will as I grew older. If I appeared in the kitchen, Harry would fly on to my head, scold and bite at me in the most alarming way, so that either he must be confined in the back premises, or *I* must retreat whence I came.

Now and then by accident the cockatoo escaped into the garden, whirling over head most provokingly while the household rushed about making frantic efforts to catch him; but even in that moment of liberty he could not resist the pleasure of frightening me, so that if I could be produced he was certain to descend, and thus fall into the hands of his pursuers.

Tom, Dick, and Harry were on the friendliest terms.

If Harry could possibly manage to escape from the kitchen to another room, he was sure to be found by the cat's side, taking with meekness the raps which were dealt out with no unsparing paw if he became too familiar in his demonstration of regard.

We had them for thirteen or fourteen years, those three special pets of ours, and each one received honourable burial in the kitchen-garden.

Dick departed first, and was encased in a neat glove-box for a coffin, his small grave being dug beneath a fine white currant-bush.

Tom's end was a sad one, for some ill-disposed person poisoned him when he was taking his walks abroad; and he suffered terribly before we put him under one of the apple-trees he had climbed so often in days of health and spirits.

Last of all I must record the decease of Harry, one I don't like to think of. We were going away at last from the old place—so far away that pets were an incumbrance, and we were trying to find a home for the cockatoo, when cook settled the difficulty for us by getting him "put out of his misery" as she called it.

It was done from a feeling of love to her troublesome pet, and no one blamed her; when he was dead she knew he was beyond the reach of neglect or unkindness, and she never would have believed that a stranger could be kind to Harry. So a third grave was made, and this time at the root of one of the peach-trees, on the sunniest side of the garden; and we left our old home without any pets at all to trouble or to please us.

Of course as time passed we had others; still no cat or bird seems quite the same to me as those I have been telling you of—the Tom, Dick, and Harry of the far-away days.

Great-Uncle Hugh.

HE was my father's uncle, though only eight years the elder of the two, so that he was a very *young* uncle when he first had a nephew, you see.

I suppose it was on this account that papa called him "Hugh," and we called him uncle. Of course he had been "Hugh" when they were at the same school for a little time— one boy eight and the other just sixteen, and "leaving."

It was not easy to imagine our great-uncle a school-boy, he was such a very old-fashioned man; he did not even dress like any one else. On Christmas Days Uncle Hugh always joined our party, and I knew exactly what his presents would be, for from the time I was six until the Christmas after I was fourteen, he always gave me a red pocket-book for the coming year and five shillings.

After I had become a young lady I expect my Christmas gift would have been the same, only by that time Uncle Hugh's seat at the long dinner-table was empty, and his name was written upon a grave-stone far away.

When he was really gone from us, we used to talk of his kind heart and funny ways with a smile and a sigh—a smile which no sorrow could quite chase away, for he was so very droll, and yet a sigh because we had lost one more of the gentle, simple souls who pass through life so quietly that one never discovers half their goodness until they have slipped out of our reach.

Everybody played tricks on Uncle Hugh, and he bore them so good-humouredly that I do believe it encouraged us all in thinking of something fresh.

I remember a time when the house was filled to overflowing, because of the wedding of one of my aunts, and one room had been kept for Uncle Hugh.

He came the evening before the marriage was to take place, and some one (I don't know which of our numerous cousins) had made a plan for depriving him of part of his night's rest.

One of those ugly "dummies," which milliners used to make bonnets and caps upon, had been found in some cupboard—a dummy with a severely proper expression upon her painted face, which suggested the idea that in a nightcap it might be supposed the face of some elderly maiden-lady visitor.

Accordingly, just before the time for every one to retire, the figure was placed in Uncle Hugh's bed, with a frilled nightcap surrounding the placid countenance, and two or three mischievous girls were tittering with ill-suppressed mirth at the thought of what would follow.

'If ever you have heard of Mr. Pickwick's adventure at the inn, or if by-and-bye you read it for yourself, you may guess in part how Uncle Hugh was distressed and embarrassed by finding himself in an occupied apartment and, above all, a lady's apartment!

Yet in his horror, his thoughtfulness for others appeared in the way he bore the misfortune. Enveloping himself in a dressing-gown, and deciding that it was too late to rouse any one to show him which *was* his room, poor Uncle Hugh descended the stairs, candle in hand, with noiseless footstep; he would spend the night upon the drawing-room sofa, where he should disturb nobody!

Of course the authors of the joke were upon the watch to see how it went off, and took care to follow Uncle Hugh downstairs, with well-assumed anxiety, to inquire if he "wanted anything."

"I have made a mistake in the room—that's all," he said mildly. "It is very stupid of me; I thought I had been told I was to sleep there. But I was wrong, there is a lady in it —it's really terrible, but she had already retired when I entered the room, and I did not notice it. I trust, however, that she was asleep; I came out as quietly as I could."

What could the culprits do but own to their misdeeds? feeling very much ashamed as they afterwards confessed. Surely any one but

Uncle Hugh would have been angry and offended! *He* watched the dummy removed from his bed with quiet satisfaction, merely saying, when the protestations of sorrow were resumed, "Never mind, my dears, young folks must have a little fun, I suppose, especially when old uncles come visiting."

Charlie led our kind old relative "a dance," as people say, when he was at home.

One habit of Uncle Hugh's was to carry a pair of thin boots ("pumps" he called them) in the pocket of his coat, which he put on as soon as he was fairly inside the hall-door. I suppose no human being would have induced the tidy old bachelor to set foot upon the carpets with soiled, travel-stained boots.

I remember once how surprised I was that Charlie watched so anxiously for Uncle Hugh to arrive, even ran out with a bustling welcome before the well-known knock was heard at the door.

Dreadful boy! he had been thinking all day that it would be a "spree" to confiscate one of the pumps, and see what came of it. Not difficult to accomplish, for Uncle Hugh carried them in the tail-pocket of his coat, and Charlie's fingers were dexterous. Quickly he possessed himself of the treasure, while our old uncle fumbled and fumbled in search of it, until at length we all went out to see what made him so long appearing.

"Nothing, nothing—yes, I'll come in directly (this in answer to an entreaty not to stop there in the cold hall), "it's only one of my pumps, I can't find it, and I am *sure* I had two when I started from home."

"Oh, never mind changing your boots," said my father; "come along, Hugh." But in vain; the habit of order was strong, and our uncle continued diving into one after another of his many pockets, but of course unsuccessfully.

"I came up from the railway in the omnibus," he said at last; "I must have dropped it in the straw. I should like to walk up to the Swan and see about it."

Now the Swan was an inn, a mile and half away, at which the omnibus remained until it was time to meet another train—a long walk on a snowy night, yet nothing would induce Uncle Hugh to change his mind, and to our great surprise Charlie volunteered to accompany him.

It was more than an hour before they returned; but Uncle Hugh was perfectly happy, for he held both " pumps " tightly in his hand. When Charlie owned to his misdeeds some weeks after, he told us that he had thrown the missing boot in among the loose straw of the omnibus while Uncle Hugh was looking about, and thus gave him the pleasure of discovery, and the happy consciousness that his long cold walk had not been taken in vain. *Then* I used to think such teasing was rather unkind; *now* I think worse of it, because I have seen the mischief which *may* result from " a practical joke."

There was a story connected with Uncle Hugh—I expect there always is one woven into the lives of people who we think so strange and eccentric, only we don't get to hear of it.

When he was just grown up and leaving school, with all the world so bright before him, his father lost the greater part of his large property, and house, land, carriages, horses were sold. It was a terrible blow to Hugh, but a worse one followed, for his father died within a month of the sale of his property—the worry killed him, they say. Poor Hugh! There was his mother left for him to care for, and two younger sisters to be educated. It was enough to make a lad like him despair, only that at heart he was so brave, though so quiet in appearance. With the help of friends he obtained a situation in a counting-house where, for his father's sake, he received a better salary than would ordinarily be given to one so young; and, laying aside all his dreams of a college course, Hugh applied himself to the dull routine of business. With the help of his mother's own little income, they managed to live in a small cottage not far from their once luxurious home, and as years went by, our uncle succeeded, by steady plodding and great self-denial, in having his sisters placed in first-rate schools.

It was thus it happened—so our parents say—that he never had a home, and wife, and little children of his own; all that could have made life bright he gave up for the sake of his mother and his sisters, but never letting them feel that there was any self-denial in it.

By the time I knew Uncle Hugh, he was alone, for his mother and one sister had died, and the other was married and away in India.

He was well off then; but the old habit of helping others was strong as ever, and all his money went in charity to those who needed it, and never for his own gratification.

When I think of our good old uncle—so simple, so generous, so thorough in his piety—it seems to me that he was surely one of those "faithful servants" to whom the Great Master will speak the blessed words, "Well done."

"Long Dresses."

FROM a very young child I had been small of my age, and as I grew older I regarded this fact in the light of a serious misfortune.

Looking at the proportions of my companions—many younger than myself, too—I envied their inches, and pondered long and seriously as to *why* I did not grow.

"I am afraid she will be short, like none of our family." That was what relations said when they came to see us after perhaps a long interval of absence, and many a time some such speech has brought tears into my eyes, I can assure you.

However, when I was about fifteen years

old, it was discovered that, in some safe sure method, I had been increasing in stature, and was really too old for short frocks.

Can I describe the joy which thrilled through my heart, or the excited happiness which kept me wakeful at night during the first week at least after the announcement. Long dresses! I could not be so short or so childish in appearance as friends and relatives affected to believe me.

I was going to a party—a juvenile party, at which I purposed helping to "amuse the little ones;" and it was settled that my first long dress should be made for this occasion.

Very simple it was—only clear white muslin, with here and there a knot of pale pink ribbon; but surely no girl about to be presented to her Majesty ever took more pride in her court train than I felt in my flowing skirts on the night of that children's party.

When I saw a vision in the glass of a tall figure in a cloud of white muslin, it did not seem "me" at all—only some one I might have met and said "How do you do?" to.

Only that morning had I packed away my doll on the upper shelf of the wardrobe, feeling very much inclined to shed tears over the separation. An hour or two before dressing for the party, I had seized upon a little girl who came to pay a call with her mamma, delighted with the excuse of amusing her with the dolls' house, for which I was considered "quite too old." Yet now I was transformed into this grown-up lady reflected in the mirror!

For several days I had practised walking with a table-cover pinned round me, so that I might the more gracefully support the dignity of tailed skirts, still I felt shy and embarrassed, as I walked downstairs, to be "looked at" by my father and mother before starting.

And so at last I was put into the carriage, my heart beating with most unwomanly fear, and filled with a strong inclination to beg Stafford to go with me to the drawing-room door, just as she had done in the old "little girl" days.

But dignity triumphed over shyness, and with as stately a step as I could possibly assume, I walked in after my name with the unpleasant consciousness that all the little people were saying inwardly, "Why, she's got on a long frock!"

It is undeniably true that my friends fought shy of me. The fact was that I must have been the oldest of the visitors, and mine therefore the only long dress, excepting, of course, one or two mammas and aunties, who counted for nothing. The little girl who had played with my dolls' house in the afternoon answered me now in a half-whisper, gazing all the while with round astonished eyes, as if I had developed into a female Chang, or some such monstrosity.

During the first half hour I neither enjoyed myself nor my dignity, but when the dancing began I forgot my long dress.

It was brought to my recollection most unpleasantly after a while though. In the last figure of a quadrille some dreadful boy caught his foot in the muslin folds, and the result was a long rent and the gathers pulled out.

Tears of vexation were in my eyes as Mrs. Ackworth took me off to her dressing-room, where I had to remain while the maid repaired the damage as best she could. The music and dancing went on, while my feet beat impatiently on the floor, and Dobson *was* such a time making me fit to reappear upon the scene of pleasure.

In bitterness of spirit I meditated upon the awkwardness of big boys of the *hobbledehoy* age, and decided that there were drawbacks in long dresses which I had never expected.

It seems now, as I look back, that the evening of Mrs. Ackworth's party was a turning-point, a corner in my life from which I started on a fresh path; at any rate my flowing dresses opened a new era in my history.

Not so very long after—only a month or two—it was decided that I should go abroad for a time with a friend of my mother's, who was taking her own young daughter for a little "polishing," as Charlie called it.

I liked, and did *not* like, the prospect. It seemed exciting and important to go to Paris, and write letters home reporting one's impressions of the gay bright city; but first there was the parting—a sad one, even though it was to be only for a year, and perhaps but six months.

Surely home scenes never seemed so fair as during those few weeks of preparation. There was such a beautiful leafiness everywhere, and the fresh showers brightened up each tiny spray in the hedgerows, and the sunbeams turned every raindrop into sparkling gold, and glanced upon the grey walls of the old church and the little white cottages which clustered round it, making everything its fairest and loveliest. On the whole I was more sorry than glad to go away—more sorry than glad to be quite sure I was no longer a little girl, but a young lady about to get the finishing touches to her home education.

What a fortunate thing it is for us all, old and young, that the bustle of getting ready and the excitement of leave-taking keeps off so much pain and regret up to the very last farewell. But it comes afterwards; it came to me as I sat by Mrs. Henderson in the carriage which drove me away from home, *en route* for the railway station at which our journey commenced. I could not talk to her, could not join in Helen's laughter; and when we were fairly crossing the Channel, and there was nothing to do but watch the rising and falling of the waves, and see the long line of white cliffs fading in the distance, I cried sorrowfully because I was so far from the dear old place and the dear old days of childhood.

I am not going to tell you of my arrival in *La belle France*, nor how my spirits rose, as a girl's spirits always do, with novelty and pleasure.

This has been a little panorama of home, in which other places and scenes have no part, so you must leave me watching the soft murmuring waves, and fortunately free from the miseries of sea-sickness, yet saying in my heart:

> "Oh for the days beyond recalling!
> Oh for the golden days!"

Selections from

R. WASHBOURNE'S CATALOGUE.

18 PATERNOSTER ROW, LONDON.

Post Office Orders to be made payable at the General Post Office.

NEW BOOKS.

The Monk of the Monastery of Yuste; or, the Last Days of the Emperor Charles V. An Historical Legend of the 16th century. From the Spanish, by Mariana Monteiro. 2s. 6d.

"It is well calculated to instruct and entertain the minds of young persons, since it is a tale of piety and also historical."—*Tablet.* "A very realistic picture of the character of Charles in monastic repose. We have read every page of the volume with much pleasure."—*Catholic Times.*

The Battle of Connemara. By Kathleen O'Meara, author of "A Daughter of St. Dominick," "Life of Frederick Ozanam," "Life of Bishop Grant." 3s.

Industry and Laziness. By Franz Hoffman. From the German, by James King. 12mo., 3s.

The Two Friends; or, Marie's Self-denial. By Madame D'Arras. 12mo., 1s.; gilt, 1s. 6d.

My Golden Days. By M. F. S. 12mo., 2s. 6d., or in 3 vols. 1s. each; or gilt, 1s. 6d.

1. Yellow Holly—The One Ghost of my Life—Dollie and I—Housekeeping Troubles—On an Island—Berengaria. 2. Tableaux Vivants—Pietro—Willie's Escape—Seaside Adventures—The Captain's Monkey—Eighty-eight—A Sprained Ankle—Dr. Syntax. 3. Wet Days—Rousseau's Dream—Nerves—Our Firsts of May—Tom, Dick and Harry—Great-Uncle Hugh——Long Dresses.

Tim O'Hallaran's Choice; or, From Killarney to New York. By Sister M. F. Clare. 3s. 6d.

To Rome and Back. Fly-leaves from a Flying Tour. Edited by W. H. Anderdon, S.J. 12mo., 2s.

"Graphic and vigorous sketches. As Father Anderdon says, truly they have their special interest, by reason of date no less than of place and scene. 'To Rome and Back' refers to Rome and Back at the time of the Papal Jubilee. It is as beautiful a celebration of that memorable event as has anywhere appeared. If only for that purpose it ought to pass at once, by right, into very wide circulation.—*Weekly Register*. "We note in the Authoress a power of condensing a description in a bold and striking metaphor. There is all a woman's quickness and keenness of perception, and a power of sympathy with the noble, the beautiful, and the true. The book unites the three characteristics not always combined in the records of travellers—justness of view, interest, and attractiveness of style." —*The Month*. "One of the most pleasant little books we have read for a long time, and is one which has peculiar attractions for Catholic readers."—*Waterford News*.

Stories of the Saints. By M. F. S. Third series. 12mo., 3s. 6d.

From Sunrise to Sunset. A Catholic Tale. By L. B. 12mo., 3s. 6d.

"A story for young readers, with a distinctly religious tendency, well written and interesting."—*The Bookseller*. "A pleasing tale, of which some of the incidents take place in the Grisons of Switzerland. There is a good power of description of scenery, in very clear grammatical language. In fact, the purity of style of L. B. is quite an example to the average novel writer."—*Public Opinion*. "A lively, chatty, pleasant little novel, which can do no harm to any one, and may afford amusement to many young persons."—*Tablet*.

Andersen's Sketches of Life in Iceland. Translated by Myfanwy Fenton. 12mo., 2s. 6d.

"In the one case they are simply pretty tales; in the other curious illustrations of the survival to our own time of thought and manners familiar to every reader of the Sagas."—*Graphic*. "Ever welcome additions to the literary flora of a primitive and little-known country, such as Iceland must still be deemed. The Princess of Wales has been pleased to accept this unpretentious little story-book, written in the high latitudes where legends flourish abundantly."—*Public Opinion*. "Told with simple eloquence. A happy mean of refreshing simplicity which every reader must enjoy."—*Catholic Times*. "The style is fresh and simple, and the little volume is altogether very attractive."—*Weekly Register*.

Rest, on the Cross. By E. L. Hervey. Author of "The Feasts of Camelot," "My Godmother's Tales from Many Lands," &c., &c. 12mo., 3s. 6d.

"This is a heart-thrilling story of many trials and much anguish endured by the heroine, whose course of true love was not destined to 'run smooth.' Rest comes to her, however, where alone it can come to all. The little tale is powerfully and vividly told."—*Weekly Register*. "Mrs. Hervey has shown a rare talent in the relation of moral tales calculated to fascinate and impress younger readers."—*Somerset County Gazette.* "An interesting and well-written religious story for young people."—*The Bookseller.* "An emotional and gushing little novelette."—*Church Times.* "It is impossible for us to know how far the events and situations are real, and how far imaginary; but if real, they are well related, and if imaginary, they are well conceived."—*Tablet.* "It is written in the gentlest spirit of charity,"—*Athenæum.*

The Feasts of Camelot, with the Tales that were told there. By Eleanora Louisa Hervey. 3s. 6d.; or separately, Christmas, 1s.; Whitsuntide, 1s.

"This is really a very charming collection of tales, told as is evident from the title, by the Knights of the Round Table, at the Court of King Arthur. It is good for children and for grown up people too, to read these stories of knightly courtesy and adventure and of pure and healthy romance, and they have never been written in a more attractive style than by Mrs. Hervey in this little volume."—*Tablet.* "This is a very charming story book."—*Weekly Register.* "Mrs. Hervey brings the great legendary hero within the reach of children, but the stories are quite sufficiently well told to deserve the perusal of more critical readers."—*The Month.* "These tales are well constructed, and not one of them is destitute of interest."—*Catholic Times.* "In the tales told at the Christmas Feasts the associations of the season are allowed full play, and the reader revels in fascinating recitals of the Christmas doings of the mighty men of old."—*Somerset County Gazette.* "King Arthur and the stories told at his court have a charm that is felt by young and old. The idea of gathering them in a book for young readers was excellent."—*Athenæum.* "Full of chivalry and knightly deeds, not unmixed with touches of quaint humour."—*Court Journal.* "The substance and spirit of Arthurian romance."—*Examiner.* "A graceful and pleasing collection of stories."—*Daily News.* "Quaint and graceful little stories."—*Notes and Queries.* "To those who wish to go back to the prehistoric days and indulge themselves in the old dream-land of romance, this is just the book."—*Guardian.* "There is a high purpose in this charming book, one which is steadily pursued—it is the setting forth of the true meaning of chivalry."—*Morning Post.*

My Godmother's Stories from many Lands. By Eleanora Louisa Hervey. Fcap. 8vo., 3s. 6d.

"Very well and, above all, very briefly told. The stories are short and varied. The Godmother's Anecdotes are very good stories."—*Saturday Review.* "A great number of short Stories and Anecdotes of a good moral tone."—*Tablet.* "A delightful fairy Godmother is this, who promises to rival the famous Princess Scheherezade as a story-teller."—*Weekly Register.* "Suitable for boys and girls of ten or twelve years, and is capable of teaching them not a few wholesome truths in an agreeable but really impressive manner."—*Illustrated London News.* "The stories are instructive and interesting."—*Thanet Advertiser.* "It is pleasant exceedingly to come across a sound, healthy, and moral and instructive story-book like the one now before us."—*Somerset County Gazette*. "Many of the stories are such as belong to the common stock of the world, and ought to be made known to the young generation."—*Guardian*. "A charming collection of tales, illustrating some great truths."—*Church Times*. "With a few exceptions each story has 'some heart of meaning in it,' and tends to kindle in the mind all that is good and noble,"—*Windsor Gazette*. "A collection of short stories, anecdotes, and apologues on various topics, delightfully told."—*Athenæum*.

A Daughter of St. Dominic. By Grace Ramsay (Kathleen O'Meara). Fcap. 8vo., 1s.; stronger bound, 1s. 6d.; cloth extra, 2s.

"A beautiful little work. The narrative is highly interesting."—*Dublin Review*. "It is full of courage and faith and Catholic heroism."—*Universe*. "A beautiful picture of the wonders effected by ubiquitous charity, and still more by fervent prayer."—*Tablet*.

A Hundred Years Ago; or, a Narrative of Events leading to the Marriage and Conversion to the Catholic Faith of Mr. and Mrs. Sidney, of Cowpen Hall, Northumberland, to which are added a few other Incidents in their Life. By their Granddaughter. Fcap. 8vo., 2s. 6d.

"Apart from all family considerations, it is full of interest. The simple language of a domestic history, which has been judiciously retained in publication, gives at once the idea of absolute truthfulness."—*The Month*. "The book is very readable and is certain to become popular."—*Catholic Times*. "We have seldom read a more charming little record than the one which has been here put together. It is very sweetly and simply written."—*Weekly Register*.

Cassilda; or, the Moorish Princess of Toledo. 2s.

Bertha; or, the Consequences of a Fault. 2s.

Captain Rougemont; the Miraculous Conversion. 2s.

The Little Hunchback. By the Countess de Ségur. With 8 full-page Illustrations. 3s.

Bessy; or the Fatal Consequence of Telling Lies. 1s.; stronger bound, 1s. 6d.; gilt, 2s.

"This is a very good tale to put into the hands of young servants."—*Tablet*. "The moral teaching is of course thoroughly Catholic, and conveyed in a form extremely interesting."—*Weekly Register*.

Stories for my Children.—The Angels and the Sacraments. Square 16mo. 1s.

Canon Schmid's Tales. New translation, with Original Illustrations, 3s. 6d. Separately: 1. Canary Bird; 2. Dove; 3. Inundation; 4. Rose Tree; 5. Water Jug; 6. Wooden Cross; 6d. each, or 1s. gilt.

R. Washbourne, 18 Paternoster Row, London.

Tom's Crucifix, and other Tales. By M. F. S. 3s.; or separately, 1s. each, or 1s. 6d. gilt.
Tom's Crucifix, and *Pat's Rosary.
Good for Evil, and Joe Ryan's Repentance.
The Old Prayer Book, & Charlie Pearson's Medal.
Catherine's Promise, and Norah's Temptation.
Annie's First Prayer, and *Only a Picture.
The Tales marked * are not in the 3s. volume.

"Simple stories for the use of teachers of Christian doctrine."—*Universe*. "This is a volume of short, plain, and simple stories, written with the view of illustrating the Catholic religion practically by putting Catholic practices in an interesting light before the mental eyes of children. The whole of the tales in the volume before us are exceedingly well written."—*Register*.

Fluffy. A Tale for Boys. By M. F. S., author of "Tom's Crucifix and other Tales." 3s. 6d.

"A charming little story. The narrative is as wholesome throughout as a breath of fresh air, and as beautiful in the spirit of it as a beam of moonlight."—*Weekly Register*. "The tale is well told, and we cannot help feeling an interest in the fortunes of Fluffy from his three months in jail to his final development as a schoolmaster."—*Tablet*.

The Three Wishes. A Tale. By M. F. S. 2s. 6d.

"A pretty neatly told story for girls. There is much quiet pathos in it and a warm Catholic spirit."—*The Month*. "We are glad to welcome this addition to the story-books for which the author is already favourably known."—*United Irishman*. "The tale is singularly interesting. The story of Gertrude with her gratified wish has about it all the interest of a romance, and will, no doubt, find especial favour."—*Weekly Register*. "Like everything which M. F. S. writes, the book is full of interest; there are pictures of an old-fashioned English home, with romping children, so natural that we seem to know both it and them; a little tale of sorrow with all the sadness of truth about it; and the history of a life to which GOD seemed to have granted a religious vocation and yet denied the means of following it."—*Tablet*. The chief heroine is a striking model of what a young woman ought to be, and may become, if animated by sincere desire."—*Catholic Times*.

Catherine Hamilton. By the author of "Tom's Crucifix," &c. Fcap. 8vo. 2s. 6d.; gilt, 3s.

"We have no doubt this will prove a very attractive book to the ittle folks, and would be glad to see it widely circulated."—*Catholic World*. "A short, simple, and well-told story, illustrative of the power of grace to correct bad temper in a wayward girl."—*Weekly Register*. "We are very much pleased with this little book. The story is simple and well-told."—*Tablet*.

Catherine grown Older. Fcap. 8vo. 2s. 6d.; gilt 3s.

"Those who are familiar with the history of Catherine in her wayward childhood will welcome with no little satisfaction this sequel to her story from the hand of the same charming writer. There is a simplicity about the style and an earnest tenderness in the manner of the narrative which renders it singularly impressive."—*Weekly Register.* "Catherine's character will delight English children."—*Tablet.*

Simple Tales. Square 16mo. cloth antique, 2s. 6d.

"Contains five pretty stories of a true Catholic tone, interspersed with some short pieces of poetry. . . Are very affecting, and told in such a way as to engage the attention of any child."—*Register.* "This is a little book which we can recommend with great confidence. The tales are simple, beautiful, and pathetic."—*Catholic Opinion.* "It belongs to a class of books of which the want is generally much felt by Catholic parents."—*Dublin Review.* "Beautifully written. 'Little Terence' is a gem of a Tale."—*Tablet.*

Terry O'Flinn. By the Very Rev. Dr. Tandy. Fcap. 8vo. 1s.; stronger bound, 1s. 6d.; gilt, 2s.

"The writer possesses considerable literary power."—*Register.* "A most singular production."—*Universe.* "An unpretending yet a very touching story."—*Waterford News.* "Excellent indeed is the idea of embodying into a story the belief that there is ever beside us a guardian angel who reads the thoughts of our hearts and strives to turn us to good."—*Catholic World.* "The idea is well sustained throughout."—*Church Times.*

The Adventures of a Protestant in Search of a Religion: being the Story of a late Student of Divinity at Bunyan Baptist College; a Nonconformist Minister, who seceded to the Catholic Church. By Iota. 3s. 6d.; cheap edition, 2s.

"Will well repay its perusal."—*Universe.* "This precious volume."—*Baptist.* "No one will deny 'Iota' the merit of entire originality."—*Civilian.* "A valuable addition to every Catholic library."—*Tablet.* "There is much cleverness in it."—*Nonconformist.* "Malicious and wicked."—*English Independent.* "An admirable and amusing, yet truthful and genuinely sparkling work. The characters are from life."—*Catholic Opinion.*

The People's Martyr, a Legend of Canterbury. 4s.

The Artist of Collingwood. By Baron Na Carriag. 2s.

Munster Firesides; or, the Barrys of Beigh. By E. Hall. 3s. 6d.

The Village Lily. Fcap. 8vo. 1s.; gilt, 1s. 6d.

"Charming little story."—*Weekly Register.*

Forty Years of American Life. By Dr. Nichols. 5s.

Fairy Tales for Little Children. By Madeleine Howley Meehan. 6d.; cloth, 1s.; stronger bound, 1s. 6d.; gilt, 2s.

"Full of imagination and dreams, and at the same time with excellent point and practical aim, within the reach of the intelligence of infants."—*Universe.* "Pleasing, simple stories, combining instruction with amusement."—*Register.* "In this little book there is the conservative propriety of virtue always conquering vice, of industry and merit triumphant, after the requisite probation and risk. So if mammas want a pretty little book to give to their imaginative young ones, this last gentle venture will suffice."—*Tablet.*

Rosalie; or, the Memoirs of a French Child. Written by herself. 1s.; stronger bound, 1s. 6d.; gilt, 2s.

"It is prettily told, and in a natural manner. The account of Rosalie's illness and First Communion is very well related. We can recommend the book for the reading of children."—*Tablet.* "The tenth chapter is beautiful."—*Universe.* "The lessons inculcated tend to improve the youthful mind. We cannot too strongly recommend the book."—*Waterford News.* "This is one of those nicely written stories for children which we now and then come across."—*Catholic World.* "Charmingly written."—*Church Herald.*

The Story of Marie and other Tales. Fcap. 8vo., 2s.; gilt, 3s.; or separately:—The Story of Marie, 2d.; Nelly Blane, and A Contrast, 2d.; A Conversion and a Death-Bed, 2d.; Herbert Montagu, 2d.; Jane Murphy, The Dying Gipsy, and The Nameless Grave, 2d.; The Beggars, and True and False Riches, 2d.; Pat and his Friend, 2d.

"A very nice little collection of stories, thoroughly Catholic in their teaching."—*Tablet.* "A series of short pretty stories, told with much simplicity."—*Universe.* "A number of short pretty stories, replete with religious teaching, told in simple language."—*Weekly Register.*

Sir Ælfric and other Tales. By the Rev. G. Bampfield. 18mo. 6d.; cloth, 1s.; gilt, 1s. 6d.

"Written in a good spirit and pleasing style."—*Westminster Gazette.* "Beautifully and touchingly written."—*Tablet.* "Written with much grace and vigour."—*Church News.* "We have no hesitation in saying that children will enjoy these tales."—*Church Times.*

Rupert Aubray. By the Rev. T. J. Potter. 3s.
Percy Grange. By the same author. 3s.
Farleyes of Farleye. By the same author. 2s. 6d.
Sir Humphrey's Trial. By the same author. 2s. 6d.
The Last of the Catholic O'Malleys. A Tale. By

M. Taunton. 18mo. cloth, 1s. 6d.; stronger bound, 2s.

"A sad and stirring tale, simply written, and sure to secure for itself readers."—*Tablet.* "Deeply interesting. It is well adapted for parochial and school libraries."—*Weekly Register.* "A very pleasing tale."—*The Month.* "Simply and naturally told."—*Freeman's Journal.*

Eagle and Dove. From the French of Mademoiselle Zénaïde Fleuriot. By Emily Bowles. Cr. 8vo., 5s.: cheap edition, 2s. 6d.

"We recommend our readers to peruse this well-written story."—*Register.* "One of the very best stories we have ever dipped into."—*Church Times.* "Admirable in tone and purpose."—*Church Herald.* "A real gain. It possesses merits far above the pretty fictions got up by English writers."—*Dublin Review.* "There is an air of truth and sobriety about this little volume, nor is there any attempt at sensation."—*Tablet.* "The subject is forcibly and ingeniously put before the reader, and the original matter in it is apt and painful."—*Derbyshire Courier.* "It is superior to the common run of stories in artistic merit, its characters and scenes have a peculiar and romantic interest, and its religious and moral tone is up to the highest mark."—*Catholic World.*

Cistercian Legends of the 13th Century. Translated from the Latin by the Rev. Henry Collins. 3s.

"A casket of jewels. Most fascinating as legends and none the less profitable for example, consolation, and encouragement."—*Weekly Register.* "The legends are full of deep spiritual teaching, and they are almost all authenticated."—*Tablet.* "Well translated and beautifully got up."—*The Month.* "Full of heavenly wisdom,"—*Catholic Opinion.* "The volume reminds us forcibly of the illustrations in the 'Christian Perfection' of Rodriguez."—*Dublin Review.*

Cloister Legends; or, Convents and Monasteries in the Olden Time. *Second Edition.* Cr. 8vo. 4s.

"Deeply interesting and edifying."—*Weekly Register.* "A charming book of tales of the olden time."—*Catholic Opinion.* "A charming volume."—*Universe.* "All more or less interesting and well told."—*Tablet.* "The stories are very well told."—*The Month.*

Keighley Hall and other Tales. By Elizabeth King. 6d.; cloth, 1s.; stronger bound, 1s. 6d.; gilt, 2s.

"The religious teaching is very good, and stamps the work as being that of a loyal member of the one true Church."—*Tablet.* "The Tales are Catholic to the backbone."—*Weekly Register.* "Interesting and well-written stories."—*Westminster Gazette.* "Very interesting as stories."—*Church News.* "Full of devotion and piety."—*Northern Press.*

Chats about the Rosary; or, Aunt Margaret's Little Neighbours. Fcap. 8vo. 3s.

"There is scarcely any devotion so calculated as the Rosary to keep up a taste for piety in little children, and we must be grateful for any help in applying its lessons to the daily life of those who already love it in their unconscious tribute to its value and beauty." —*Month*. "We do not know of a better book for reading aloud to children, it will teach them to understand and to love the Rosary."—*Tablet*. Illustrative of each of the mysteries, and connecting each with the practice of some particular virtue."—*Catholic Opinion*. "This pretty book carries out a very good idea, much wanted, to impress upon people who do not read much the vivid picture or story of each mystery of the Rosary."—*Dublin Review*.

Margarethe Verflassen. Translated from the German by Mrs. Smith Sligo. Fcap. 8vo. 3s.; gilt, 3s. 6d.; cheap edition, 1s. 6d.

"A portrait of a very holy and noble soul, whose life was passed in constant practical acts of the love of God."—*Weekly Register*. "It is the picture of a true woman's life, well fitted up with the practice of ascetic devotion and loving unwearied activity about all the works of mercy."—*Tablet*. "Those who may wish to know something about Convent life will find it faithfully pourtrayed in every important particular in the volume before us. We cordially commend it to our readers."—*Northern Star*.

A Romance of Repentance; or, the Heroine of Vesuvius. A remarkable sensation of the Seventeenth Century. By Rev. Dr. O'Reilly. 3s. 6d.

Ned Rusheen. By the Poor Clares. Crown 8vo. 6s.

The Prussian Spy. A Novel. By V. Valmont. 4s.

Sir Thomas Maxwell and his Ward. By Miss Bridges. Fcap. 8vo. 1s.

"A charming little story of home griefs and loves. The characters are admirably well discriminated."—*Weekly Register*. "Nor is brevity the only or chief merit of the book. A high tone of religious feeling prevails."—*Tablet*.

Adolphus; or, the Good Son. 18mo. gilt, 6d.

Nicholas; or, the Reward of a Good Action. 6d.

The Lost Children of Mount St. Bernard. Gilt, 6d.

The Baker's Boy; or, the Results of Industry. 6d.

The Truce of God: a Tale of the Eleventh Century. By G. H. Miles. 4s.

Tales and Sketches. By Charles Fleet. 8vo. 2s.; stronger bound, 2s. 6d.; gilt, 3s. 6d.

"Pleasingly written and containing some valuable hints.... There is a good deal of nice feeling in these short stories."—*Tablet*. "Well written; they will be found innocent as well as pleasant reading."—*Weekly Register*.

The Journey of Sophia and Eulalie to the Palace of True Happiness. Translated by the Rev. Father Bradbury, Mount St. Bernard's. Fcap. 8vo. 3s. 6d.; cheap edition, 1s. 6d.

"The book is essentially suited to women, and especially to those who purpose devoting themselves to the hidden life of sanctity. It will prove, however, a useful gift to many young ladies whose lot is in the world."—*Weekly Register.* "This mode of teaching imparts an extraordinary degree of vividness and reality."—*Church Review.* "Unquestionably the book is one that for a certain class of minds will have a great charm."—*The Scotsman.* "No one can weary with the perusal, and most people will enjoy it very much."—*Tablet.*

The Fisherman's Daughter. By Conscience. 4s.
The Amulet. By Hendrick Conscience. 4s.
Count Hugo of Graenhove. By Conscience. 4s.
The Village Innkeeper. By Conscience. 4s.
Happiness of being Rich. By Conscience. 4s.
Ludovic and Gertrude. By Conscience. 4s.
The Young Doctor. By Conscience. 4s.
Margaret Roper. By A. M. Stewart. 6s.; gilt, 7s.
Limerick Veteran. By the same. 5s. and 6s.
Life in the Cloister. By the same. 3s. 6d.
Alone in the World. By the same. 4s. 6d.
Festival Tales. By J. F. Waller. 5s.
The Victims of the Mamertine. Scenes from the Early Church. By Rev. A. J. O'Reilly, D.D. 5s.
Revelations of Ireland. 1s.
Story of an Orange Lodge. 1s.
The Kishoge Papers. Tales of Devilry and Drollery. 1s. 6d.
Chances of War. An Irish Tale. By A. Whitelock. 5s.
Diary of a Confessor of the Faith. 12mo., 1s.
The Pale and the Septs. A Romance of the Sixteenth Century. By Emelobie de Celtis. 6s.
Pearl among the Virtues. By Rev. P. A. De Doss. 12mo., 3s.
· Recollections of the Reign of Terror. By the Abbé Dumesnil. 2s. 6d.
A Broken Chain. 18mo. gilt, 6d.
Silver Teapot. By Elizabeth King. 18mo., 4d.
The First Christmas for our dear little ones. By Miss Mulholland. 15 Illustrations, 4to. 5s.

Legends of the Saints. By M. F. S., author of "Stories of the Saints." Square 16mo., 3s. 6d.

"A pretty little book, couched in studiously simple language."—*Church Times.* "A number of short legends, told in simple language for young readers by one who has already given us two charming volumes of 'Stories of the Saints.'"—*Tablet.* "Here we have more than fifty tales, told with singular taste, and ranging over a vast geographical area. Not one of them will be passed over by the reader."—*Catholic Times.* "A delightful boon for youthful readers."—*Weekly Register.* "It is got up in the most attractive as well as substantial style as regards binding, paper, and typography, while the simple and beautiful legends are told in a graceful and flowing manner, which cannot fail to rivet the attention and interest of the youthful reader."—*United Irishman.*

Stories of the Saints. By M. F S., author of "Tom's Crucifix, and other Tales," "Catherine Hamilton," &c. 3 series, each 3s. 6d., gilt, 4s. 6d.

"As lovely a little book as we have seen for many a day."—*Weekly Register.* "Interesting not only for children but for persons of every age and degree."—*Tablet.* "A great desideratum. Very pleasantly *written.*"—*The Month.* "A very attractive volume. A delightful book."—*Union Review.* "Admirably adapted for reading aloud to children, or for their own private reading."—*Catholic Opinion.* "Being full of anecdotes, they are especially attractive."—*Church Herald.* "Well selected."—*Dublin Review.*

Stories of Holy Lives. By M. F. S. Fcp. 8vo., 3s. 6d.

"The stories seem well put together."—*The Month.* "It sets before us clearly and in simple language the most striking features in the character and history of many whose very names are dear to the hearts of Catholics."—*Tablet.*

Stories of Martyr Priests. By M. F. S. 12mo., 3s. 6d.

"It contains the sad and yet glorious histories of more than thirty sufferers amongst the Roman Catholic Clergy."—*Pilot.* "The stories are briefly and simply narrated."—*Church Times.* "The stories are written with the utmost simplicity, and with such an earnest air of reality about every page that the youthful reader may forget that he has a book in his hand, and can believe that he is 'listening to a story.'"—*Weekly Register.* "It has been the task of the writer, while adhering strictly to historical facts, to present the lives of these Christian heroes in a pleasing and attractive form, so that, while laying before the youthful mind deeds as thrilling as any to be found in the pages of romance, a chapter in her history is laid open which is at once the glory and the shame of England."—*United Irishman.* "Short memoirs well written and which cannot fail to attract not only 'the Catholic Boys of England,' to whom the book is dedicated, but also all the men and women of England to whom the Catholic faith is dear."—*Tablet.* "Sad stories of over thirty Priests who perished for conscience sake."—*Catholic Times.* "No lives of great men can depict so glorious a picture as these Stories of Martyred Priests, and we trust they will be read far and wide."—*Dublin Review.*

The Story of the Life of St. Paul. By M. F. S., author of "Legends of the Saints," &c., &c. Fcap. 8vo., 2s. 6d.

"A most attractive theme for the prolific pen of the author of 'Tom's Crucifix and other Tales.'"—*Weekly Register.* "The author knew instinctively how to present the incidents most effectively, and has made the most of them."—*Catholic Times.*

The Panegyrics of Fr. Segneri, S.J. Translated from the original Italian. With a preface by the Rev. Fr. W. Humphrey, S.J. Crown 8vo., 5s.

The Immaculate Conception. The Blessed Virgin. St. Joseph. St. John the Evangelist. St. John Baptist. St. Stephen. St. Ignatius of Loyola. St. Francis Xavier. St. Aloysius Gonzaga. St. Thomas of Aquin. St. Philip Neri. St. Antony of Padua. The Blessed Sacrament. The Holy Winding Sheet. The Angel Guardian.

Albert the Great: his Life and Scholastic Labours. From original Documents. By Professor Sighart. Translated by Rev. Fr. T. A. Dixon, O.P. With a Photographic Portrait. 8vo., 10s. 6d.; cheap edition, 5s.

"All this, and more, are recorded in the volume now before us, which goes to make up one of the most interesting religious biographies recently issued from the Catholic press."—*Irish Monthly.* "A translation of Dr. Sighart's 'Albertus Magnus' will be welcome in many quarters. The volume is admirably printed and beautifully got up, and the frontispiece is a valuable engraving of B. Albert's portrait after Fiesole."—*Dublin Review.* "Albert the Great is not well known . . . yet he is one of those pioneers of inductive philosophy whom our modern men of science cannot without black ingratitude forget. His memory should be dear not only to those who value the sanctity of life, but to those also who try, as he did, to wrest from nature the reason of her doings."—*The Month.* "The volume is a large one, as befits the subject, and it carries the reader through most of the scenes of Albert's life with a graphic power which does honour to the literary skill of Fr. Dixon. . . . We certainly recommend this book as worthy a place in every library."—*Catholic Times.* "The fullest record that has ever been penned of one of the grandest luminaries in the history of the Church."—*Weekly Register.* "The book is extremely interesting, full of information, and displays great powers of research and critical judgment. . . . The details are most interesting in themselves and valuable in their historical research. The volume is eminently worth perusal."—*Tablet.*

Lives of the Saints for every Day in the Year. Translated from M. Didot's edition. Beautifully printed on thick toned paper, with borders from ancient sources, scarlet cloth gilt, gilt edges, 4to. 21s.

Lives of the First Religious of the Visitation of Holy Mary. By Mother Frances Magdalen de Chaugy. With two Photographs. 2 vols., cr. 8vo. 10s.

S. Vincent Ferrer, of the Order of Friar Preachers: his Life, Spiritual Teaching, and practical Devotion. By Fr. Pradel. Translated by Fr. Dixon, O.P. With a Photograph. 5s.

Butler's Lives of the Saints. 2 vols., 8vo., cloth, 28s.; or in cloth gilt, 34s.; or in 4 vols., 8vo., cloth, 32s.; or in cloth gilt, 48s.; or in leather gilt, 64s.

Life of S. Bernardine of Siena. With a portrait, 5s.

Life of S. Philip Benizi. With a portrait, 5s.

Life of S. Veronica Giuliani, and Blessed Battista Varani. With a portrait, 5s.

Life of S. John of God. With a portrait, 5s.

Life of B. Giovanni Colombini. By Feo Belcari. Translated from the editions of 1541 and 1832. with a Photograph. Cr. 8vo. 3s. 6d.

Sketch of the Life and Letters of the Countess Adelstan. By E. A. M., author of "Rosalie, or the Memoirs of a French Child," "Life of Paul Seigneret," &c. 1s.; stronger bound, 2s. 6d.

"The great interest of the book, even above the story of the conversion of her husband, is the question of education. The essay on the bringing up of children and the comparative merits and demerits of Convent and home education, is well worth the careful study both of parents and those entrusted with the task of instruction."—*The Month.* "Her judgments are always wise."—*Catholic Opinion.* "We can safely recommend this excellent little biographical sketch. It offers no exciting interest, but it is calculated to edify all."—*Tablet.*

Life of Paul Seigneret, Seminarist of Saint-Sulpice. 6d.; cloth, 1s.; stronger bound, 1s. 6d.; gilt, 2s.

"An affecting and well-told narrative... It will be a great favourite, especially with our pure-minded, high-spirited young people."—*Universe.* "We commend it to parents with sons under their care, and especially do we recommend it to those who are charged with the education and training of our Catholic youth."—*Register.*

Life of Sister Mary Cherubina Clare of S. Francis, Translated from the Italian, with Preface by Lady Herbert. Cr. 8vo. with Photograph, 3s. 6d.
Life and Letters of Sir Thomas More. By A. M. Stewart. Illustrated, 8vo., 10s. 6d.; gilt, 11s 6d.
Life of Gregory Lopez, the Hermit. By Canon Doyle, O.S.B. With a Photograph. 12mo., 3s. 6d.
St. Angela Merici. Her Life, her Virtues, and her Institute. From the French of the Abbé G. Beetemé. 12mo., 4s. 6d.
Life of St. Columba, &c. By M. F. Cusack. 8vo., 6s.
Life and Prophecies of S. Columbkille, or Columba, 3s. 6d.
Recollections of Cardinal Wiseman, &c. By M. J. Arnold. 2s. 6d.
Life of St. Augustine of Canterbury. 12mo. 3s. 6d.
Life of St. German. 12mo. cloth, 3s. 6d.
Life of Stephen Langton. 12mo. cloth, 2s. 6d.
Prince and Saviour. A Life of Christ for the Young. By Rosa Mulholland. 6d. Illustrated, 2s. 6d.
Life of S. Paul of the Cross. By the Passionist Fathers. 3s.
Nano Nagle. By Rev. W. Hutch, D.D. 7s. 6d.
Life of St. Boniface. By Mrs. Hope. 6s.
Life of the Ven. Anna Maria Taigi. From the French of Calixte, by A. V. Smith Sligo. 2s. 6d.; stronger bound, 5s.
Venerable Mary Christina of Savoy. 6d.
Memoirs of a Guardian Angel. Fcap. 8vo. 4s.
Life of St. Patrick. 12mo. 1s.; 8vo., 6s.; gilt, 10s.
Life of St. Bridget, and of other Saints of Ireland. 1s.
Insula Sanctorum: the Island of Saints. 1s.; cloth, 2s.
Sufferings of Our Lord. With Introduction by Dr. Husenbeth. Illustrated. 5s.
Life, Passion, Death, and Resurrection of Our Blessed Lord. Translated from Ribadeneira. 1s.
Glory of St. Vincent de Paul. By Cardinal Manning. 1s.
Life of S. Edmund of Canterbury. From the French of the Rev. Father Massé, S. J. 1s. and 1s. 6d.

Life of St. Francis of Assisi. From the Italian of St. Bonaventure. By Miss Lockhart. With a Photograph, 3s. 6d.
Patron Saints. By Eliza Allen Starr. Illustrated. Crown 8vo. 10s.
Life of Cardinal Wiseman; with full account of his Obsequies. 1s.; cloth, 1s. 6d.
Life of Count de Montalembert. By G. White. 6d.
Life of Mgr. Weedall. By Dr. Husenbeth. 1s.
Pius IX: his early Life to the Return from Gaeta. By Rev. T. B. Snow, O.S.B. 6d.
Life of Pope Pius IX. 6d. Cheap edition, 1d.
Challoner's Memoirs of Missionary Priests. 8vo. 6s.

BY SISTER MARY FRANCES CLARE.

O'Connell: his Life and Times. 2 vols., 18s.
The Liberator: his Speeches and Letters. 2 vols., 18s.
Life of Father Matthew. 2s. 6d.
Life of Mary O'Hagan, Abbess, Poor Clares. 6s.
Life of St. Joseph, 6d., cloth, 1s.; Life of St. Patrick, 6d., cloth, 1s.; 8vo., 6s.; gilt, 10s.
Life of St. Patrick. Illustrated by Doyle. 4to. 20s.
The History of the Blessed Virgin. By the Abbé Orsini. Translated by Dr. Husenbeth. With eight Illustrations. Crown 8vo. 3s. 6d.
Our Blessed Lady of Lourdes: a Faithful Narrative of the Apparitions of the Blessed Virgin. By F. C. Husenbeth, D.D. 18mo. 6d.; cloth, 1s.; with Novena, 1s.; cloth, 1s. 6d. Novena, separately, 4d.; Litany, 1d., or 6s. per 100. Medal, 1d.
Devotion to Our Lady in North America. By the Rev. Xavier Donald Macleod. 8vo. 5s.

"The work of an author than whom few more gifted writers have ever appeared among us. It is not merely a religious work, but it has all the charms of an entertaining book of travels. We can hardly find words to express our high admiration of it."—*Weekly Register.*

Life of the Ever-Blessed Virgin. Proposed as a Model to Christian Women. 1s.
The Victories of Rome. By Rev. Fr. Beste. 1s.

The History of the Italian Revolution. The Revolution of the Barricades. (1796—1849.) By the Chevalier O'Clery, M.P., K.S.G. 8vo. 7s. 6d.; cheap edition, 3s. 6d.

"The volume is ably written, and by a man who is acquainted with the subject about which he writes."—*Athenæum*. "Mr. O'Clery will be satisfied with the honour of having accomplished a good work.... He has done his duty well enough, as any one who chooses to get the book for himself can see."—*Fun*. "Well-written, and contains many passages that are marked by candour and amiability."—*Guardian*. "Mr. O'Clery's graphic and truthful narrative.... Written in an easy flowing style, the volume is by no means heavy reading."—*Pilot*. "It was a happy thought on the part of Mr. O'Clery to conceive the possibility of contributing something towards the removal of the existing ignorance; and it was better still to have girded himself up to the task of giving execution to his thought in the very able and satisfactory manner in which he has done his work."—*The Month*. "The author grasps the whole subject of the Revolution with a master mind.... From the first page to the last it is of absorbing interest."—*Catholic Times*. "It is the only well digested summary in the English tongue of all the reliable records bearing on the events of which it treats."—*Nation*. "The narrative virtually covers the whole of the Papacy, or, in other words, Christianity, since the date of the foundation, nineteen centuries ago."—*Weekly Register*. "Written with the calmness of the historian, yet with something of the energy of faith, this book cannot fail to be most interesting to Catholics, while it should do good service among Protestants. The style is easy and enjoyable."—*Tablet*. "In every line of the book we find a vigour and freshness of mind, combined with a maturity of judgment on the great question at issue."—*Wexford People*.

Two Years in the Pontifical Zouaves. By Joseph Powel, Z.P. With 4 Engravings. 8vo. 3s. 6d.

"It affords us much pleasure, and deserves the notice of the Catholic public."—*Tablet*. "Familiar names meet the eye on every page, and as few Catholic circles in either country have not had a friend or relative at one time or another serving in the Pontifical Zouaves, the history of the formation of the corps, of the gallant youths, their sufferings, and their troubles, will be valued as something more than a contribution to modern Roman history."—*Freeman's Journal*.

Rome and her Captors. Letters collected and edited by Count Henri d'Ideville, and translated by F. R. Wegg-Prosser. Cr. 8vo. 4s.

"The letters describe the attempted capture of Rome by Garibaldi; and the tissue of events which brought about in 1870 the seizure of Rome by Victor Emanuel."—*Dublin Review*. "A series of letters graphically depicting the course of political events in Italy, and showing in its true light the dishonesty of the Piedmontese government, the intrigues of Prussia, and the ill-treatment to which the Pope has been subjected. We most cordially recommend the volume to our readers."—*Church Herald*. "One of the most opportune contributions that could be made to popular literature."—*Cork Examiner.* "We have read the book carefully, and have found it full of interest, whether from its own intrinsic merits or from the ease of the translation we care not to enquire."—*Catholic Opinion.* "At the time of its publication it occasioned no little stir on account of its vivid portraiture of character, its keen observation, and its sententious remarks."—*Hereford Journal.* "The translator of this wonderfully interesting volume has done a distinct good."—*Weekly Register.*

Personal Recollections of Rome. By W. J. Jacob, Esq., late of the Pontifical Zouaves. 8vo. 1s. 6d.

"An interesting description of the Eternal City... The value of the Pamphlet is enhanced by a catena of authorities on the Temporal Power."—*Tablet.* "All will read it with pleasure, and many to their profit."—*Weekly Register.* "We cordially recommend an attentive perusal of Mr. Jacob's book."—*Nation.*

A General History of the Catholic Church: from the commencement of the Christian Era until the present time. By Abbé Darras. 4 vols., 48s.

The First Apostles of Europe. The 2nd Edition of "The Conversion of the Teutonic Race." By Mrs. Hope. 2 vols. crown 8vo. 10s.

"Mrs. Hope has quite grasped the general character of the Teutonic nations and their true position with regard to Rome and the world in general... It is a great thing to find a writer of a book of this class so clearly grasping and so boldly setting forth truths, which familiar as they are to scholars, are still utterly unknown—or worse than unknown, utterly misconceived—by most of the writers of our smaller literature."—*Saturday Review.* "A brilliant and compact history of the Germans, Franks, and the various tribes of the former Jutes, Angles, and Saxons, who jointly formed the Anglo-Saxon, or, more correctly, English people... Many of the episodes and notices of the Apostolic Missionaries, as well as the general story, are very happily and gracefully conveyed."—*Northern Star.* "This is a real addition to our Catholic literature."—*Tablet.* "In the first place it is good in itself, possessing considerable literary merit; then it fills up a blank, which has never yet been occupied, to the generality of readers, and lastly and beyond all, it forms one of the few Catholic books brought out in this country which are not translations or adaptations from across the Channel. It is a growth of individual intellectual labour, fed from original sources, and fused by the polish of a cultivated and discerning mind."—*Dublin Review.* "Mrs. Hope's historical works are always valuable."—*Weekly Register.* "A very valuable work... Mrs. Hope has compiled an original history, which gives constant evidence of great erudition, and sound historical judgment."—*The Month.* "This is a most taking book: it is solid history and romance in one."—*Catholic Opinion.* "It is carefully, and in many parts beautifully written, and the account of the Irish monks is most instructive and interesting.."—*Universe.*

Holy Places; their Sanctity and Authenticity. By the Rev. Fr. Philpin. With Maps. Crown 8vo. 6s.; cheap edition, 2s. 6d.

"Fr. Philpin weighs the comparative value of extraordinary, ordinary, and natural evidence, and gives an admirable summary of the witness of the early centuries regarding the holy places of Jerusalem, with archæological and architectural proofs. It is a complete treatise of the subject."—*The Month.* "The author treats his subject with a thorough system, and a competent knowledge. It is a book of singular attractiveness and considerable merit."—*Church Herald.* "Dean Stanley and other sinners in controversy are treated with great gentleness. They are indeed thoroughly exposed and refuted."—*Register.* "Fr. Philpin has a particularly nervous and fresh style of handling his subject, with an occasional picturesqueness of epithet or simile."—*Tablet.*

Spalding's (Archbp.) Works. Miscellanea, 2 vols., 21s.; Protestant Reformation, 2 vols., 21s.; Evidences of Catholicity, 10s. 6d.

Men and Women of the English Reformation, from the days of Wolsey to the death of Cranmer. By S. H. Burke, M.A. 2 vols., 12mo., 10s. *nett.* Vol. II. can be had separately, price 5s.

The chief topics of importance in the second volume are: Archbishop Cranmer's opinions upon Confession; The Religious Houses of Olden England; Burnet as a Historian; What were Lord Cromwell's Religious Sentiments? Effects of the Confiscation on the People; The Church and the Holy Scriptures; Death-bed Horrors of Henry VIII.; Scenes upon the Scaffold—Lady Jane Grey's heroic Death; The Rack and the Stake; The Archbishop condemned to be Burnt Alive—Awful Scene; A General View of Cranmer's Life.

"A clever and well-written historical statement of facts concerning the chief actors of our so-called Reformation."—*Month.* "Interesting and valuable. The author has hit on the true way of writing history attractively, by making it a series of biographies connected together and mutually interdependent. His combination of the descriptions of contemporary, with the opinions and remarks of modern, writers, such as Sharon Turner, and Froude, who are generally cited only to be refuted, has imparted a tone of liveliness and freshness which is much needed by the subject matter of the book."—*Tablet.* "Contains a great amount of curious and useful information, gathered together with evident care, and, we think, with great fairness. The author is intent upon giving us facts. He has evidently examined the authorities on which the history of these times must depend with the most laudable diligence. He gives us much valuable information, and a good deal which, to ourselves at least, is new."—*Dublin Review.* "A clear picture of the villains and the villanies that were busy about the work of the

Devil in the sixteenth century in this country. The author produces evidence that cannot be gainsaid,"—*Universe.* " Full of interest, and seems to be very temperately written."—*Church Review.* "The book supplies many hitherto unknown facts of the times of which it is to be a history."—*Church Opinion.* " A certain and most important era of British history has been fortunate in finding in Mr. Burke all the qualifications requisite for the task he has undertaken. We may fairly assert that the facts in the book have been collected at a trouble and cost few but the author himself can appreciate. Moreover, they have been given to the public in a dress simple but effective with all the charm that word painting exercises on the imagination, in order to recall to existence the actors of bygone days. Indeed, Mr. Burke's pictures of the Men and Women of the Reformation are life-like, and, in a certain sense, we might call them *tableaux vivants.* The reader must certainly be colour-blind who cannot perceive the strict adherence to truth he exhibits in the colouring of his characters. He exposes to public view the corrupt heart of Henry VIII., the irreligious motives of Anne Boleyn, the hypocrisy of Cranmer, the wit of Erasmus, the temporising policy of Gardner, the sacrilegious robbery of Cromwell, the weakness of Wolsey, the sublime faith of Fisher, the integrity of More, and the queenly dignity of Katherine of Aragon. In doing full justice to the heroic conduct of the Carthusians and the Observant Fathers, he contrasts their noble character with that of the Reformers and their wives, and heightens the effect with touches of the sharpest irony. But nowhere is he more at home than when he seems to revel in exposing the blunders of Froude, whose partiality and whose inconsistency he establishes by the strongest proof taken from Froude's own writings. All the while he treats his adversary in the fairest conceivable spirit, giving him a full hearing, so that the genuine worth of the verdict against his opponent is the more apparent. But if we admire any one thing more than another in this publication, it is the immense research visible on every page, and which is evidently the labour of years. From every quarter information has been obtained, and nothing has been extenuated, nor aught set down in malice."—*Weekly Observer and Northern Advocate.* " It is, in truth, the only dispassionate record of a much-contested epoch we have ever read. It is a work of which writer and publisher may feel proud, and both, as far as these volumes go, have supplied a want to which Mr. Disraeli once referred—'The History of England has yet to be written.'"—*Cosmopolitan.* " Mr. Burke collects and arranges his facts, states them lucidly, and lays them before the public in just such a tone and temper as befit a judge who is summing up a trial and delivering a charge to the jury. A spirit of candour characterises the whole work."—*Nation.*

BY ARTHUR AND T. W. M. MARSHALL.

Comedy of Convocation in the English Church. Edited by Archdeacon Chasuble, D.D. 2s. 6d.

The Oxford Undergraduate of Twenty Years Ago :

his Religion, his Studies, his Antics. By a Bachelor of Arts. 2s. 6d. ; cloth, 3s. 6d.

"The writing is full of brilliancy and point."—*Tablet*. "It will deservedly attract attention, not only by the briskness and liveliness of its style, but also by the accuracy of the picture which it probably gives of an individual experience."—*The Month*.

The Infallibility of the Pope. A Lecture. 8vo. 1s.

"A splendid lecture, by one who thoroughly understands his subject, and in addition is possessed of a rare power of language in which to put before others what he himself knows so well."—*Universe*. "There are few writers so well able to make things plain and intelligible as the author of 'The Comedy of Convocation.'... The lecture is a model of argument and style."—*Register*.

Reply to the Bishop of Ripon's Attack on the Catholic Church. 6d.

The Harmony of Anglicanism. Report of a Conference on Church Defence. 2s. 6d.

"'Church Defence' is characterised by the same caustic irony, the same good-natured satire, the same logical acuteness which distinguished its predecessor, the 'Comedy of Convocation.'.'. A more scathing bit of irony we have seldom met with."—*Tablet*. "Clever, humorous, witty, learned, written by a keen but sarcastic observer of the Establishment, it is calculated to make defenders wince as much as it is to make all others smile."—*Nonconformist*.

The above 5 Vols. in one, cloth, price 6s.

Dramas, Comedies, Farces.

St. William of York. A Drama in Two Acts, for boys. 6d.
Major John André. An Historical Drama (Boys.) 2s.
He would be a Lord. Comedy in Three Acts. (Boys.) 2s.
St. Louis in Chains. Drama in Five Acts, for boys. 2s.
Shandy Maguire. A Farce for boys in Two Acts. 2s.
The Duchess Transformed. A Comedy in One Act, for girls. By W. H. A. 6d.
The Reverse of the Medal. A Drama in Four Acts, for young ladies. 6d.
Ernscliff Hall: or, Two Days Spent with a Great-Aunt. A Drama in Three Acts, for young ladies. 6d.
Filiola. A Drama in Four Acts, for young ladies. 6d.
The Convent Martyr. By Dr. Husenbeth. 2s.
Shakespeare. Expurgated edition. By Rosa Baughan. 6s. Comedies, in a separate volume, 3s. 6d.
Road to Heaven. A game for family parties, 1s. & 2s.

www.ingramcontent.com/pod-product-compliance
Lightning Source LLC
Chambersburg PA
CBHW020916230426
43666CB00008B/1475